C000293096

BRADSHAW'S GUIDE TO THE RAILWAYS OF WALES

Volume Seven

John Christopher and
Campbell McCutcheon

AMBERLEY

Left: Cliché or heritage, the image of traditional Welsh costume featured on countless souvenirs, such as this postcard, aimed at the tourist market. On this card a flap opens to reveal a string of little photographs of the area. The name of the town would be over-printed to serve a variety of different locations. In the nineteenth century the railways were the major factor in the flourishing of the tourist industry in Wales.

About this book

This book is intended to encourage the reader to explore many aspects of the railways of Wales. Through Bradshaw's account and the supportive images and information it describes the history of the railways, their engineering works, architecture and some of the many changes that have occurred over the years. Hopefully it will encourage you to delve a little deeper when exploring the railways and other works, but please note that public access and photography are sometimes restricted for reasons of safety and security.

First published 2015

Amberley Publishing
The Hill, Stroud
Gloucestershire, GL5 4EP

www.amberley-books.com

Copyright © John Christopher and Campbell McCutcheon, 2015

The right of John Christopher and Campbell McCutcheon to be identified as the Author of this work has been asserted in accordance with the Copyrights, Designs and Patents Act 1988.

ISBN 978 1 4456 3851 5
EBOOK 978 1 4456 3855 3

All rights reserved. No part of this book may be reprinted or reproduced or utilised in any form or by any electronic, mechanical or other means, now known or hereafter invented, including photocopying and recording, or in any information storage or retrieval system, without the permission in writing from the Publishers.

British Library Cataloguing in Publication Data.
A catalogue record for this book is available from the British Library.

Typeset in 9.5pt on 12pt Celeste.
Typesetting by Amberley Publishing.
Printed in the UK.

Bradshaw in Wales

The stupendous iron Railway Bridge by which the line is carried over the river Wye, is one of the most remarkable in the country. Bridges of this size are so rare that we think it right to direct the attention of the reader to this one. Mr Stephenson's magnificent Britannia Bridge displays one method of crossing wide spans. The Chepstow bridge of Mr. Brunel is another mode, and shows, as might have been expected, his peculiarly original and bold conception, accompanied by extraordinary economy, by arranging his materials in the form of a large suspended truss, and attaching the roadway to suspended chains kept in a state of rigidity by vertical trusses or struts, inserted between the chains and a circular wrought iron tube, spanning the river, 309 feet in length.

Bradshaw's description of the tubular railway bridge at Chepstow is interesting for several reasons. Most notably, because he refers to Isambard Kingdom Brunel by name, but also because it is the point at which the South Wales Railway – later to be absorbed within the Great Western Railway – crosses over the Wye from England and enters the Principality of Wales.

This is the seventh volume in the Amberley series of books based on *Bradshaw's Descriptive Railway Hand-Book of Great Britain and Ireland*, which was originally published in 1863. Bradshaw's guides were aimed at the general traveller and were not written from an engineering perspective. Having said that, Bradshaw was right

Below: To cross the Wye at Chepstow, Brunel used an innovative tubular girder design.

on the button in his admiration of the railway bridge at Chepstow and in identifying Brunel's strongest characteristics, saying that the bridge shows 'his peculiarly original and bold conception'. George Bradshaw and I. K. Brunel were close contemporaries who both enjoyed considerable success in their chosen fields and died while relatively young. Bradshaw, born in 1801, died in 1853 at the age of fifty-two, while Brunel who was born just a few years later in 1806, was fifty-three years old when he died in 1859.

It was Brunel and his fellow engineers who drove the railways, with their cuttings, embankments and tunnels, through a predominantly rural landscape to lay the foundations of the nineteenth-century industrial powerhouse that has shaped the way we live today. It is fair to say that the railways are the Victorians' greatest legacy to the twentieth and twenty-first centuries. They shrank space and time. Before their coming different parts of the country had existed in local time based on the position of the sun, with Bristol, for example, running ten minutes behind London. The Great Western Railway changed all that in 1840, when it applied synchronised railway time throughout its area. The presence of the railways defined the shape and development of many of our towns and cities, they altered the distribution of the population and forever changed the fundamental patterns of our lives. For many millions of Britons the daily business of where they live and work, and how they travel between the two, is defined by the network of iron rails laid down nearly two centuries ago by the great engineers and an anonymous army of railway navvies.

The timing of the publication of Bradshaw's guidebooks is interesting. This particular account is taken from the 1863 edition of the handbook although, for practical reasons, it must have been written slightly earlier, probably between 1860 and 1862. By this stage the railways had lost their pioneering status, and with the heady days of the railway mania of the 1840s over they were settling into the daily business of transporting people and goods. By the early 1860s the GWR's mainline from London to Bristol, for example, had been in operation for around twenty years and was still largely in its original as-built form. It was also by this time that rail travel had become sufficiently commonplace to create a market for Bradshaw's guides.

As a young man George Bradshaw had been apprenticed to an engraver in Manchester in 1820, and after a spell in Belfast he returned to Manchester to set up his own business as an engraver and printer specialising principally in maps. In October 1839, he produced the world's first compilation of railway timetables. Entitled *Bradshaw's Railway Time Tables and Assistant to Railway Travelling*, the slender cloth-bound volume sold for sixpence. By 1840 the title had changed to *Bradshaw's Railway Companion* and the price doubled to one shilling. It then evolved into a monthly publication with the price reduced to the original and more affordable sixpence.

Although George Bradshaw died in 1853, the company continued to produce the monthly guides and in 1863 it launched *Bradshaw's Descriptive Railway Hand-Book of Great Britain and Ireland* (which forms the basis of this series of books). It was originally published in four sections as proper guidebooks without any of the timetable information of the monthly publications. Universally referred to simply as 'Bradshaw's Guide', it is this guidebook that features in Michael Portillo's *Great*

George Bradshaw and the men of iron

As with the great Victorian engineers, George Bradshaw's fame and prosperity grew with the rapid spread of the railways. Bradshaw, Brunel and Robert Stephenson were close contemporaries – they were born and also died only a few years apart – although there is no record of Bradshaw, shown left, having met either of the engineers. Having previously ignored Brunel's Royal Albert Bridge at Saltash – *Vol. 1: Paddington to Penzance* – Bradshaw makes up for it this time when writing about the tubular bridge at Chepstow.

Above: An engraving of Isambard Kingdom Brunel based on a studio photograph. Brunel was a close friend of Robert Stephenson, who is shown on the left. They died within months of each other, marking the end of an era in the world of British engineering. The other engineer referred to by Bradshaw, because of his suspension bridges at Conwy and Menai, was Thomas Telford. A great builder of roads, Telford was of a previous generation.

THE FIRST "BRADSHAW"

A reminiscence of Whitsun Holidays in Ancient Egypt. From an old-time tabl(e)ature

Above: Punch's take on the ubiquitous Bradshaw guides and timetables.

British Railway Journeys, and as a result of its exposure to a new audience the book found itself catapulted into the best-seller list almost 150 years after it was originally published.

Without a doubt the Bradshaw Guides were invaluable in their time and they provide the modern-day reader with a fascinating insight into the mid-Victorian rail traveller's experience. In 1865 *Punch* had praised Bradshaw's publications, stating that 'seldom has the gigantic intellect of man been employed upon a work of greater utility'. Having said that, the usual facsimile editions available nowadays don't make especially easy reading with their columns of close-set type. There are scarcely any illustrations for a start, and attempts to trace linear journeys from A to B are interrupted by distracting branch line diversions. That's where this volume comes into its own. *Bradshaw's Guide to the Railways of Wales* takes the reader on a a series of journeys, starting with South Wales – an area dominated by the influence of Brunel of course – from Chepstow all the way to Pembrokeshire and also including the numerous branches into the valleys. Then comes a section on Central Wales, although it should be noted that the Cambrian Railway, the main mover in this area, was not incorporated until 1864, a year after the original guide's publication. The final section begins in England at Chester and then heads westward to Conwy, Bangor and on to the island of Anglesey via Stephenson's magnificient Britannia Bridge over the Menai Straits.

The illustrations show scenes from Victorian times and they are juxtaposed with new photographs of the locations as they are today. The accompanying information provides greater background detail on the railways, the great bridges, and the many locations along the route. Please note that Bradshaw's place names and spellings have been preserved as they appeared in the original 1863 text.

Crossing the River Severn

Above: As engineer to the Bristol & South Wales Union Railway, Brunel built a ferry pier at New Passage to connect with Portskewett and the junction of the South Wales Railway. *Below right:* The Severn Railway Bridge was completed in 1879, but collapsed in 1960 after being struck by barges in dense fog. *Below left and bottom right:* Two views of the Severn Tunnel, one showing repairs being carried out underwater after a flooding during construction, and one of the portal. It was completed in 1886 and remains the main link with South Wales.

South Wales

Chepstow to Newport

CHEPSTOW

POPULATION, 3,364. Distance from station, ¼ mile. A telegraph station. HOTEL
– Beaufort Arms. FLYS etc. – Fare to Tintern Abbey and back, time not exceeding
eight hours, carriage and pair for seven persons, 16s; driver and gates 6s; for ten
persons, 20s and 6s. Fly for two persons, 8s and 3s 6d per mile. Single horse, 1s.
MARKET DAYS – Wednesday and Saturday, and last Monday in each month.
FAIRS – Monday before March 1st, Whit Friday, June 22nd, August 1st, Friday on
or before Oct. 29th.

Chepstow is a market town, in the county of Monmouth, situated near the mouth
of the river Wye. The town is large and has within the last few years been much
improved. It was formerly surrounded by walls, and defended by a castle.

Excursionists visit Tintern Abbey, Wyndcliffe, and Chepstow Castle, which are
thus described in Mr Cliffe's *Guide Book of South Wales*:

Tintern Abbey – The graceful Wye, filled up to its banks, and brimming over with
the tide from the Severn Sea, glides tranquilly past the orchards and fat glebe of
'Holy Tynterne.' On every side stands an amphitheatre of rocks, nodding with hazel,
ash, birch, and yew, and thrusting out from the tangled underwood high pointed
crags, as it were, for ages the silent witness of that ancient Abbey and its fortunes;
but removed just such a distance as to leave a fair plain in the bend of the river, for
one of the most rare and magnificent structures in the whole range of ecclesiastical
architecture. As you descend the road from Chepstow, the building suddenly bursts
upon you, like a gigantic stone skeleton; its huge gables standing out against the sky
with a mournful air of dilapidation. There is a stain upon the walls, which bespeaks
a weather-beaten antiquity; and the ivy comes creeping out of the bare, sightless
windows; the wild flowers and mosses cluster upon the mullions and dripstones, as
if they were seeking to fill up the unglazed void with nature's own colours. The door
is opened – how beautiful the long and pillared nave – what a sweep of graceful
arches, how noble the proportions, the breadth, the length, and the height.

The Castle is a noble and massive relic of feudalism; the boldness of its site, on a
rock overhanging the river, the vastness of its proportions, render it a peculiarly
impressive ruin. The entrance is a fine specimen of Norman military architecture:
the chapel is one of the most elegant structures ever built within a house of defence.
It was originally founded almost immediately after the Conquest.

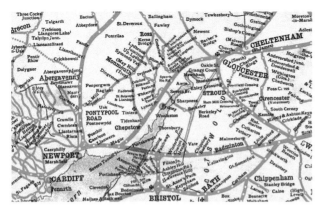

Chepstow

On the western side of the River Wye the line enters Monmouthshire and the old market town of Chepstow. Famed for its imposing castle, the 1863 *Bradshaw* comments that the town has 'within the last few years been much improved.'

Above: Whether you enter Chepstow by rail or on the A48 road bridge, you can't fail to be impressed by the castle ruins overlooking the Wye. Construction commenced in Norman times. It fell into disuse as a garrison in the late seventeenth century and within a hundred years it had become a 'picturesque' ruin. It is now a tourist attraction under the care of Cadw, the body with responsibility for historic sites within Wales. *(LoC)*

Right: The High Street, Chepstow.

The **Wyndcliffe** rises in the background of the view, from the road out of Chepstow to Monmouth. Having ascended the crag, the eye ranges over portions of nine counties, yet there seems to be no confusion in the prospect; the proportions of the landscape, which unfolds itself in regular, yet not in monotonous succession, are perfect; there is nothing to offend the most exact critic in picturesque scenery. The 'German Prince,' who published a tour in England in 1826, and who has written the best description of the extraordinary view which Wyndcliffe commands – a view superior to that from Ehrenbreitstein on the Rhine – well remarks that a vast group of views of distinct and opposite character here seem to blend and unite in one!

The stupendous iron Railway Bridge by which the line is carried over the river Wye, is one of the most remarkable in the country. Bridges of this size are so rare that we think it right to direct the attention of the reader to this one. Mr Stephenson's magnificent Britannia Bridge displays one method of crossing wide spans. The Chepstow bridge of Mr Brunel is another mode, and shows, as might have been expected, his peculiarly original and bold conception, accompanied by extraordinary economy, by arranging his materials in the form of a large suspended truss, and attaching the roadway to suspended chains kept in a state of rigidity by vertical trusses or struts, inserted between the chains and a circular wrought iron tube, spanning the river, 309 feet in length. The railway having to cross a rapid and navigable river without interruption to vessels, the Admiralty very properly required that the span over the mid channel should not be less than 300 feet; and that a clear headway of 50 feet above the highest known tide should be given. The bridge is 600 feet long; there are three spans over the land of 100 feet each, which are supported upon cast iron cylinders, six feet in diameter, and one and a quarter inch thick. These were sunk to an average depth of 48 feet through numerous beds of clay, quicksand, marl, etc., to the solid limestone rock, which was found to dip at an angle of forty-five degrees; it had therefore to be carefully levelled horizontally, and the cylinders bedded level. These were then sunk by excavating them within, and pressing them down with heavy weights, in doing which very great difficulties were overcome – immense volumes of fresh water were tapped, requiring a thirty-horse engine to pump them out. They were, when finally filled with concrete, composed of Portland Cement, sand, and gravel, which is set in a few days, as hard as a rock. The concrete is filled up to the level of the roadway, so that, should the cylinder decay, it might be taken out and replaced in sections in safety.

There are six cylinders at the west end of the main span; upon those a standard, or tower of cast iron plates, 50 feet high, is erected. A similar tower of masonry is built at the east end, on the rocky precipice of the Wye.

On the west standard is a cross girder of wrought iron, and upon which the tubes rest. The tubes serve to keep apart and steady the towers; and to their ends are attached the suspending chains. Now, in an ordinary suspension bridge, the chains hang in a festoon, and are free to move according to the limited weights passing under them; but this flexibility would be inadmissible in a railway bridge, and the continuity of the bridge would be destroyed if a very small deflection took place when passed over by a heavy locomotive. With a view to give the necessary rigidity,

Brunel's Bridge

Above: Two views of the bridge over the Wye at Chepstow, an especially awkward site with cliffs on one side and marshy ground on the other. *Right:* By the 1950s it had become too weak to deal with the increasingly heavy trains. It was dismantled in 1962 and replaced by an underslung girder bridge. The A48 road bridge was completed in 1988.

Mr Brunel introduced at every third part a stiff wrought iron girder, connecting firmly the tube to the roadway girders; and, with the aid of other adjusting screws, the suspension chains are pulled or stretched as nearly straight as possible. Other diagonal chains connect these points, so that at whatever part of the bridge an engine may be passing, its weight is distributed all over the tube and chains by these arrangements. The tube is strengthened within by the introduction of diaphragms or discs at every 30 feet, which render it both light and stiff. The bridge cost £65,420; and required 1,231 tons of wrought, and 1,003 tons of cast iron. The bridge has been visited by a great number of engineers from all countries; indeed, it is only by a personal inspection that the numerous ingenious contrivances and arrangements can be understood. The whole seems to be very simple, yet engineers fully enter into the complexity of the design, and the minute and carefully proportioned scantlings given to every past. We would especially call their attention to the cast iron ring or circle attached to the ends of the tube to prevent collapse; to the wedges introduced under the vertical trusses to adjust the exact tension upon the chain; to the curve given to the tubes themselves, increasing their strength; and to the rolling-boxes under the vertical trusses, by which means the road girders are maintained in a position to expand or contract, independently of the movements of the main tubes.

Scenery of the Wye – The Wye rises in the Plinlimmon Mountains, in the heart of South Wales, and winds along the borders of several counties, past Builth, Hay, Hereford, Ross, Monmouth, to the Bristol Channel, below Chepstow; a course of 130 miles, through scenes of great beauty and celebrity. The *Upper Wye* reaches down to Hay, on the borders of Herefordshire; after which, that portion which crosses the county is rather tame; but at Ross the *Lower Wye* begins, and ends at Chepstow. 'The former (says Mr Cliffe, in his *Book of South Wales*) has not been estimated as it deserves, because it is off the beaten track; but the opening of the railroads to Hereford (in 1853) has brought the charming scenery of the *Upper Wye* within easy reach.' It is a rapid stream, occasionally swollen by deep floods, running between high rocky banks all the way.

From *Llangurig*, which is ten miles from its source, the river rushes through deep glens and ravines, past the junction of the Dernol, and the Nanerth cliffs (three miles long) to *Rhayader-Gwy*, i.e., the Falls of the Gwy (the Welsh name of this river), so called from a cascade made by the river, close to the bridge. It stands among mountains, and has some fragments of a castle. Within a few miles is Llyn Gwyn, in which croaking trout are caught. Hence to Builth is fourteen miles. The Elan, Clarwen, and Ithon join before you reach Builth, the last at Pont-ar-Ithon, a fine spot. The Ithon may be ascended to *Llandrindod Spa*, where there are excellent saline, sulphur, and iron springs, in a healthy, though unattractive spot, with a pump-house.

Builth, is a fine part of the river, has remains of a castle, and a long bridge. Trout and salmon fishing; fine scenery. Just above it, the *Irvon* joins; it should be ascended for its charming scenery to *Llanwrtyd Wells* (fourteen miles) and *Llandovery* (twenty-three miles). When Llewellyn was hemmed in by the English under Mortimer, in Edward I's reign, he tried to get assistance to disguise his movements from the Welsh garrison of Builth Castle. It was in winter, and he had his horse's shoes reversed; this,

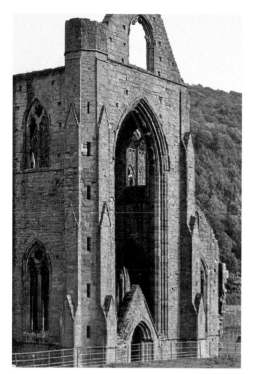

Tintern and the Wye Valley

The River Wye is the fifth-longest in the UK. Dominating this part of the valley is the dramatic 'stone skeleton' of Tintern Abbey. 'The building suddenly bursts upon you, its huge gables standing out against the sky with a mournful air of dilapidation.' *Top right:* Seen from across the river, *c.* 1890. *(LoC)* The signal box and station are relics of the Wye Valley Railway. *Below:* The Seven Sisters overlooking the river at Symonds Yat, on the edge of the Forest of Dean.

however, was revealed to the English by the blacksmith. The garrison refused to help him, and as he was retreating up the Ithon, he was surprised and killed. *Bradwyr Buallt* is the designation applied to Builth to this day. The Welsh prince was killed at Cwm-Llewellyn, near the Park Wells; and the body buried at Cefn-y-bedd, a mile or two further on the Llandovery road. There are two roads down the Wye from Builth, the highest road being on the west side; but the east road is the most interesting, especially about Aberedw, which lies in a beautiful defile, where the Ebw falls in, opposite Erwood. The castle was Llewellyn's hunting seat. Near it is the church on a cliff, a hole in which is Llewellyn's cave. Further on the Machwy (Little Wye) joins; it should be followed a little way to the Pwll Dwu or Black Rock, and its waterfall, 40 feet down. Then comes *Llangoed Castle* (J. Macnamara, Esq.), on the Brecon side, and *Boughrood* (an old castle), on the Radnor side, which commanded the old ford here. Brecon is eight miles from this, and from that place the fine scenery of the Usk may be descended. The Hatterel, or Cradle mountains, to the right are 2,545 feet high.

Glasbury, fifteen miles from Builth. Three Cocks, a good inn. *Gwyrnefed* is Colonel Wood's seat. W. Wilkins took the name of De Winton nearly twenty years ago, and *Maeslwch Castle* is the property of Captain De Winton.

Hay, four miles from here, is an old Norman town, founded by Bernard Newmarch; part of the castle remains, which was destroyed by Owen Glyndwr. It is exactly on the borders of three counties. Here the Upper Wye scenery ends. Barges are able to reach this point. *Clifford Castle,* three miles from Hay, was the birthplace of Fair Rosamund Clifford. It was built by the Conqueror's kinsman, Fitz-Osbourne.

PORTSKEWET, MAGOR, and LLANWERN stations.

NEWPORT

A telegraph station. HOTEL – King's Head; West Gate.
MARKET DAYS – Wednesday and Saturday.
FAIRS – 14 days before Holy Thursday, August 15th, Nov. 6th, Holy Thursday.

This is a sea port town of some importance, having a population of 23,249. It has a constant steam packet communication with Bristol and various parts of South Wales; and by means of its ready access by railway with the many iron districts in the neighbourhood, its traffic in that mineral, as well as coal, of late years has greatly increased. With the exception of the church, which presents various styles of architecture, the town itself has no prepossessing attractions. The scenery from the church-yard is very imposing, taking in, as it does, a wide expanse of country, as well as an extensive view of the Severn. Outside the town a stone bridge of five arches crosses the river Usk. It was erected at a cost of something over £10,000.

Newport to Cardiff

From Newport, we pass through a short tunnel and cross the river Ebw, soon after arriving at Marshfield Station, situated in a dreary extent of country, called the Westloeg Level. Crossing the river Rumney, we enter ...

Newport
Built in 1906, Newport's transporter bridge, *right,* is one of three surviving examples in the UK. They were built over waterways where it was important to provide adequate clearance for high-masted ships. The others are at Middlesbrough and Warrington.

Above: At the dawn of the industrial age this small fishing town at the mouth of the River Usk was transformed into one of the biggest docks in the country. These were mainly used for the movement of coal as well as iron and steel from the South Wales foundries.

Right: Commercial Street, Newport.

Cardiff

The medieval castle was much admired by the Victorians and during the nineteenth century the castle and mansion were remodelled in a Gothic revival style. Cardiff Castle is now run as a tourist attraction and many events have been held in its grounds including military tattoos and musical performances. A new interpretation centre was opened in 2008. *(LoC)*

Above: This 1844 print shows the view southwards across the town with the tall masts of the ships in the dock visible beyond the roof tops.

Right: GWR map of the railway network in South Wales, published by the company in the 1920s. Note the dense web of branch lines serving the many mines and foundries.

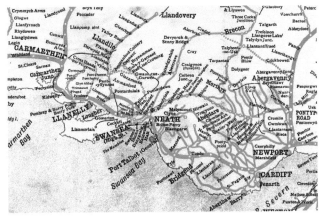

Cardiff Central is the largest and busiest station in South Wales, and the eleventh busiest in the UK outside of London. It also happens to be an extremely fine example of art deco architecture. Built of silvery grey Portland stone, between 1932 and 1934, its wide frontage bears the Great Western Railway name with a sense of permanence that has long outlived the company itself. Initially called Cardiff Station, it became Cardiff General in 1924 and then Cardiff Central in 1973. The airy booking hall is lit by an array of angular art deco lamps, and the signage on the stairwells and passageways leading to the platforms is picked out in a rich brown on the relief tiling. While the station building might not be of Bradshaw's vintage, it would not look out of place as the backdrop in one of Hercule Poirot's adventures. In 2014 work was due to start on a £200 million regeneration scheme to increase train capacity in Cardiff and the surrounding area.

GLAMORGANSHIRE

One of the most southern counties in Wales, by far the largest and most beautiful in the principality, and generally considered the garden of Wales.

The mountains are not so high as those in many of the surrounding counties, but their extreme abruptness imparts an air of wildness and elevation which greatly exceeds the reality. But what principally distinguishes this county is the profusion of coal, iron, and lime-stone, with which everywhere abounds. These mineral riches have raised Glamorganshire to great importance during the last half century. Immense establishments have been erected in the wildest part of the country; canals and roads have been formed, at great expense, to connect them with the coast; and these circumstances, reacting over the whole district, and even far beyond it, have spread the influence of improvement throughout – the facilities of intercourse creating new sources of industry.

CARDIFF

POPULATION, 32,954. A telegraph station.
HOTELS – Cardiff Arms, Angel. MARKET DAY – Saturday.
FAIRS – Second Wednesday in March, April, and May, June 29th, September 19th, and November 30th.

Cardiff, a borough town, and capital of Glamorganshire, is built on the east bank of the river Taff or Tay, near its entrance into the mouth of the Severn. The inhabitants carry on a considerable trade with Bristol, and export a great quantity of wrought iron and coal to foreign parts.

The new Bute Docks, made on a tract of waste land, by the Marquis of Bute, who is lord of the manor, are about one mile below the town, deep enough for ships, with a basin of one and a half acres, and an entrance 45 feet wide. A ship canal 1,400 yards long, 67 yards wide, runs up to the town. The coal and iron of Merthyr Tydvil and the neighbourhood are the chief exports, and the quantity almost doubles itself every two or three years.

There are remains of the town walls, with the Norman keep, 75 feet high, of the *Castle,* in which Robert Curthose (i.e., short legs), died in 1133, he having been imprisoned there for life by his brother, Henry I. The parish church is very old, and has a good tower. The new *Town Hall,* just built by H. Jones, is a handsome Italian pile, 175 feet long, including a police court, judges' and other rooms, and a *nisi prius* court. There is also a large county gaol.

Within a short distance are – *Hensol,* which belonged to Lord Chancellor Talbot; and *Wenvoe Castle,* the seat of R. Jenner, Esq., with a front of 374 feet.

[Cardiff branch on Taff Vale line – see page 55]

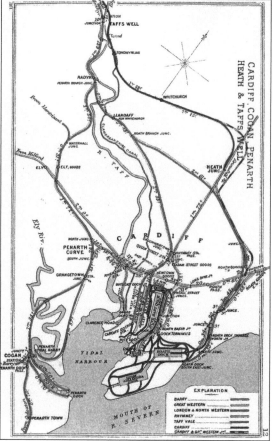

Above: The station at Bridgend opened on 18 July 1850, and although later extended, it is an original Brunel design. The footbridge was added in 1877. Both are Grade II listed.

Left: Railway chart from 1911 showing the tangle of lines into the busy Cardiff, Cogan and Penarth docks – the main shipping points for the huge quantities of coal coming from the South Wales coalfields.

Below: Lines of coal trucks at the Penarth docks with the 'tippler' towers used to load the coal onto colliers.

Cardiff To Neath

Our onward progress from Cardiff brings us through Ely, St Fagans, and Peterston, to

LLANTRISSANT

POPULATION, 5,492. Distance from station, 1½ miles.
Telegraph station at Bridgend, 9 miles.

At a distance of eight and a half miles is the market town of *Cowbridge* and its ancient well-endowed grammar school; and five miles beyond is situated *Froumon Castle*, the seat of Oliver Jones, Esq.: it belonged to the St Johns of Bletsoe, and Colonel Jones, the regicide, and contains a beautiful portrait of Cromwell.

PENCOED station.

BRIDGEND

A telegraph station. HOTELS – Wyndham Arms; Railway. MARKET DAY – Saturday. BANKERS – Sub Branch of National Provincial Bank of England.

Five miles from this improving town, at which the county elections are held, lies situated, on the coast, *Dunraven Castle* (anciently called Dindryfan, and the residence of Caractacus), the beautiful and romantic seat of the Dowager Countess of Dunraven, the heiress of the late Thomas Wyndham, Esq., who represented the county of Glamorgan in Parliament for upwards of forty years.

PYLE station.

PORT TALBOT

A telegraph station. HOTELS – Talbot Arms, and Railway.
MONEY ORDER OFFICES at Neath.

Three miles distant is *Margam Park*, the seat of C.R.M. Talbot, Esq., M.P., the descendant of the Mansells. Here is an orangery, 327 feet by 81, which contains the produce of a cargo from Holland, intended for Queen Mary, but wrecked here in 1694. A bay tree, 60 feet high, and 45 in diameter, spread, and a magnificent forest of oak trees, for which the Government in 1800 offered £40,000.

BRITON FERRY station.

NEATH

POPULATION, 6,810. A telegraph station. HOTEL – Castle.
MARKET DAY – Wednesday. FAIRS – Last Wednesday in March, Trinity Thursday, July 31st, September 12th, and last Wednesday in October.

Neath, is a coal and mining port, with an ancient castle, and some abbey ruins. Here the fine Vale of Neath may be ascended to the beautiful waterfalls at its summit *(see Merthyr Tydvil, page 55)*.

Above: Postcard, *c.* 1910, with a general view of Cardiff looking southwards.

Below right: The opening of the Swansea & Neath Railway with the first train shown passing Neath Abbey Station. The S&NR was operated by the Vale of Neath Railway, which went from Neath to Merthyr Tydfil. The S&NR line gave the railway company much-needed access to Swansea docks. Opened in September 1851, it was amalgamated with the GWR in February 1865.

Left: Traditional Welsh costume. *(LoC)*

Neath to Merthyr

From Neath we again turn out of our course, and pass the stations of Aberdylais, Resolven, and Glyn Neath. From this point, *Craig-y-linn,* the highest mountain in Glamorganshire, with its lakes and ravines, and which here makes a bold horse-shoe sweep, raising its huge bulk against the sky, may be reached.

HIRWAIN, junction of line to Aberdare, LLYDCOED, and ABERNANT stations follow, arriving at

MERTHYR TYDVIL.
[See page 55.]

South Wales Continued

Neath To Llanelly

Llansamlet station

LANDORE (SWANSEA JUNCTION)

Here passengers change carriages for Swansea, two miles distant. The view they obtain here of the valley down to Swansea is very striking. If at night, the lurid glare from countless coke ovens – if by day, the dense clouds proceeding from hundreds of chimney stalks overhanging the valley, and at all times, the arsenical sulphurous vapour filling the air, and which you may both smell and taste, give the scene a character scarcely to be seen elsewhere.

SWANSEA

A telegraph station. HOTELS – Mackworth Arms, and Castle.
Races in September. Regatta in July. MARKET DAYS – Wednesday and Saturday. FAIRS – Second Saturday in May, August 15th, October 8th, July 2nd, second Saturday after October 8th.
BANKERS – Branch Bank of England; Branch of Glamorgan Banking Co.; and West of England.

This important seat of the *copper trade,* is also a parliamentary borough (one member), jointly with Neath, etc., and stands at the head of a fine bay, on the west side of *Glamorganshire,* 216 miles from London, by the Great Western and South Wales Railways, population, 41,606. No copper ore is found in this part of Wales, but coal being abundant, it is brought hither from Cornwall and foreign countries to be fluxed. For this purpose, six-sided calcines, 17 to 19 feet long, and oval furnaces, 11 feet long, are used in the copper works, of which eight are here, on the river Pauley, or by the sea-side; one employing 500 to 600 men. The earliest was established about 1720, after the Cornish tinners began to take notice

The Landore Viaduct

Brunel used timber extensively for the construction of bridges and viaducts at a time when strong Baltic pine was readily available. Shown left and below, the viaduct at Landore, near Swansea, was the longest of these wooden structures and had a central span of 100 feet. A similar design was also used at Newport.

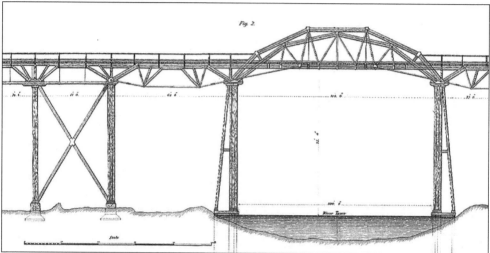

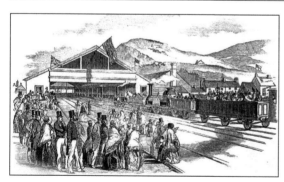

Swansea Station

Built by the South Wales Railway, later amalgamated with the GWR, the station at Swansea opened in 1850. It wasn't originally on the main line and until 1879 passengers connecting to London or Fishguard had to change at Landore, two miles to the north. The present frontage was completed in 1934, and is shown in a GWR publicity photograph from that time, *lower left*. For most of its existence the station was known as Swansea High Street, and following the closure of Swansea Victoria in the 1960s this was shortened to Swansea. The modern bilingual Welsh/English signage says Abertawe/Swansea.

of copper, which hitherto they had thrown away. The ore or shiff goes through various processes, such as calcining and melting, calcining the coarse metal, which leaves about one-third copper; then melting this to fine metal, leaving three-fifths or more than half copper; calcining the fine metal; melting the same to pigs of coarse copper, which gives nine-tenths pure metal; and lastly, roasting for blistered copper and refining it into cakes for use, which are 18 inches by 12. In this way a yearly average of 20,000 tons of copper are smelted here, from the ore brought not only from Cornwall, but from America and Australia, valued at about one and a half million sterling.

Swansea being at the mouth of the Tawe or Towey, is called Abertawe or *Abertowy* by the Welsh. By running out two piers into the bay, one being 18,000 feet long, a good harbour has been enclosed, but it is dry at low water; and floating docks are constructed. About 18,000 tons of shipping belong to this port. A castle was built here by the Normans, of which a massive quadrangular tower remains, and presents an object of some beauty. Beneath it is the Post Office, a building in the medieval style, recently erected. A large Market House, built in 1830, is 320 feet long. There are three churches, but the only one deserving notice is the parish church of St Mary, which was rebuilt in the last century. Some of the numerous chapels are well built. The public Assembly Rooms and Infirmary are handsome edifices. The *Royal Institution of South Wales* was established in 1835, and contains an important library of works relating to Welsh history, with a museum of coal, fossils, antiquities, etc. This was the headquarters of the British Association at their visit in 1854. Besides works for copper smelting, there are others for tin, zinc, pottery, etc.; all fostered by the abundance of coal and lime raised in the neighbourhood. Anthracite coal, chiefly for steamers, abounds here,

Below: Tram 51 is the only vehicle to be seen in Oxford Street, Swansea.

Swansea railways
The Rhondda
& Swansea Bay
Railway connected
the coal mines of the
Rhondda Valley with
the Swansea Bay
ports.

Top left: On 29
November 1865 a
train of the Vale
of Neath Railway
plunged from a
box girder bridge
at Swansea's North
Dock. The driver and
stoker were killed in
the accident.

Middle left: It is hard
to imagine anyone
offering a jigsaw of a
dock nowadays. This
magnificent wooden
jigsaw shows
the new docks at
Swansea. Produced
by the Chad Valley
company for the
GWR in 1924.

Bottom left: Swansea
Docks is the
collective name for
several docks to
the east of the city
centre. Like many
of the big docks,
Swansea had its own
stable of shunters.
This is a Swansea
Harbour Trust 0-4-0T.

and was used by the whole of the British steam fleet reviewed in the Solent by Her Majesty Queen Victoria, on April 23rd, 1856. Gower, the poet, and Beau Nash were born at Swansea. The river Towey runs up the vale to the Black Mountains at its head, parallel to the canal. *Skelly Park* is the seat of Sir J. Morris, Bart. *Penllergur,* J. Llewellyn, Esq. Several other seats overlook the west side of the bay, and the fine sandy beach, two or three miles long, terminating at Oystermouth, a pretty little bathing place, with an old Norman castle, near the Light or Mumbles Head. Hence the county runs out in a peninsula, much resembling in size, shape, and character, that in the south west of Milford Haven. *Gower* is the name, or *Gwyr* in Welsh, signifying crooked; it is a mass or rugged limestone, traversed by a red sandstone ridge, which is 584 feet high, at *Cefn Bryn*, where there is a cromlech called Arthur's Stone. At the Conquest it was settled by various Norman knights, and the Flemings and Somersetshire men in their train. Round the castles they built at Swansea, Penrice, Ruich, Rhosili, and Loughor, their descendants are distinct from the aborigines to this day. There are similar in the county of Wexford. The poet Gower's family were natives of this part. Druid stones, old castles, and encampments, frequently occur in this country. The cliffs and caves along the coast deserve attention; while the Worm's Head, at the west extremity, near Rhosili Bay, is a scene of awful grandeur in bad weather. It is so called from the shape of the cliffs which run out three quarters of a mile long, dipping and rising like a great sea serpent (or worm). Under the very extremity, which is 200 or 300 feet high, there is a vast funnel cave. The scenery of Swansea Bay is so beautiful that it is universally styled by both natives and tourists, 'The Bay of Naples in miniature.' Aberafon or Port Talbot, a bustling mining town, near which is *Margam Abbey*, the seat of C.R.M. Talbot, Esq., M.P., beautifully wooded, and remarkable for its orangery and gardens. There are remains of an abbey of the 12th century. Further on are Ogmore and Dunraven Castles, etc.

Gower Road (Mumbles) and Loughor stations.

Leaving the Loughor Station, we cross by a low bridge the Loughor river, and enter

CARMARTHENSHIRE

Which is mountainous and woody. The air is mild and salubrious, and the whole county is remarkably healthy and fertile. Coal and limestone are found in great abundance.

LLANELLY

POPULATION, 11,446. Distance from station, ½ mile.

A telegraph station. HOTELS – Falcon; Ship and Castle; and Thomas Arms.

MARKET DAY – Saturday. FAIRS – Holy Thursday, July 29th, September 30th, and November 10th.

LLANELLY RAILWAY AND DOCKS

Swansea Bay

Two romanticised views of the bay, including Mumbles Rock with its lighthouse, shown *above*. The two-tier lighthouse was completed in 1794, and is still in use with solar panels powering the lantern and emegency monitoring equipment.
Below: The GWR Ocean Express, a double-header, racing through South Wales with passengers from the Cunard ships at Fishguard.

Llanelly to Llandilo and Llandovery

Again turning to the right from Llanelly, we pass through Dock, Bynea, Llangennech, Pontardulais, and Pantyffynon.

CROSS INN and GARNANT stations, on a short branch to the right.

LLANDEBIE, DERWYDD ROAD, and FAIRFACH STATIONS.

LLANDILO

A telegraph station. HOTEL – Cawdor Arms. MARKET DAY – Saturday.

FAIRS – Feb. 20th, May 6th, every Tuesday, from May 14th to June 21st, Monday before Easter, August 23rd, Sept. 28th, Nov. 12th and 22nd, and Monday before Dec. 25th.

Talley Road and Glanrhyd stations.

LLANGADOCK

A telegraph station. MARKET DAY – Thursday.

FAIRS – January 16th; March 12th; May, last Thursday; June 9th; September 1st; Thursday after the 11th; December 11th.

POPULATION – 2,189; many engaged in the production of limestone and coal, which prevail in this district.

Lampeter Road station.

LLANDOVERY

POPULATION, 1,855. A telegraph station. MARKET DAYS – Wednesday and Saturday. FAIRS – January 1st, Wednesday after the 17th; March 19th; Whit-Tuesday; July 13th; October, Wednesday after the 10th; November 26th.

This straggling little town is surrounded by hills, which to the northward begin to assume a very wild and barren aspect. Here are the remains of a castle, destroyed by Cromwell.

South Wales Main Line Continued.

Llanelly to Milford Haven.

PEMBREY

POPULATION, 4,145. Telegraph station at Llanelly, 4 miles.

MARKET DAY – Saturday.

KIDWELLY

Telegraph station at Llanelly, 9 miles. HOTEL – Pelican.

MARKET DAY – Saturday. FAIRS – May 24th, August 1st, and Oct. 29th.

This is a small decayed borough, having a population of about 1,652, engaged principally as tin workers – it has also a very limited export trade. *Kidwelly Castle*

Above: No. 4 *Kidwelly* was an o-6-o tank built in 1903 by the Avonside Engine Co. for the Burry Port & Gwendraeth Railway. It passed into British Railways ownership, and was withdrawn in 1953.

Kidwelly
Above: The castle at Kidwelly. Bradshaw describes it as 'a small decayed borough'. *(LoC)*

Carmarthen Junction
Right: From 1852, a contemporary engraving of the opening of the South Wales Railway at Carmarthen Junction Station, on the mainline from Swansea to Neyland. Although the station buildings are shown in the illustration, they had not been completed by the opening date.

is here situated: it is reported to have been erected by William de Landres, a Norman adventurer, who conquered Glamorganshire about the year 1094. It now belongs to the Earl of Cawdor. The gateway is good, and altogether presents a noble relic of ancient magnificence. Here King John took refuge whilst at war with the barons.

Ferryside Station.

CARMARTHEN

A telegraph station. HOTELS – Ivy Bush, and Boar's Head.

MARKET DAYS – Wednesday and Saturday.

FAIRS – April 15th, June 3rd, July 10th, August 12th, Sept. 9th, Oct 9th, and Nov. 14th.

CARMARTHEN is the capital of *Carmarthenshire*, on the South Wales Railway, and the river Towey, with a population of 9,993, who, jointly with Llanelly, return one member. It is one of the most healthy towns, and commands a view of one of the finest vales in the principality. It has a good foreign and coasting trade; and boasts of a handsome town hall and market house, a Presbyterian college, free grammar school, &c &c. A column to the memory of Sir T. Picton, who represented the borough in parliament, stands on the west of the town, near the old Guildhall; also the Assembly Rooms, with a beautiful front built of freestone, in which are Reading Rooms, supported by public subscriptions. General Nott (to the memory of whom a handsome monument in bronze has been erected in Nott Square), together with Lewis Bailey, Bishop of Bangor, and author of the 'Practice of Piety,' were natives. The shire prison is on the castle site. A large *diocesan training school* for South Wales occupies 10 acres, and has a Gothic front of 200 feet long. In the old church is a monument to *Sir R. Steele*, who married Miss Scurlock, of Ty Gwyn, and died at the Ivy Bush, in King Street, to whom the Inn is reported to have belonged; the effigy of Rhys ap Thomas; with a good copy of the Transfiguration. Shipping of a small class come up to the quay; the harbour is three miles lower down, near the bay, which makes a fine semi-circular sweep, seventeen miles across. On the east side are the wild limestone cliffs of Worm's Head, 300 feet high, singularly shaped, and on the other Tenby, a beautiful watering place, near the lighthouse on Caldy Island.

ST CLEARS

Telegraph station at Carmarthen, 8½ miles. HOTELS – Railway, and Swan.

MARKET DAY – Saturday. FAIRS – May 4th, June 1st, Oct. 12th.

This is a mere nominal borough and market town, with a population of 1,129, engaged in the coasting and provision trade. There are the remains of a Norman castle and priory, given to All Soul's College, Oxford.

The line now leaves Carmarthen, and enters PEMBROKESHIRE.

Left: Opening of the South Wales Railway at the Narberth Road Station in Haverfordwest. Traditional costume is much in evidence. There are very few records of the costume dating from before 1770, when the first tourists started coming to Wales.

Below: The first of the GWR Ocean Express special trains leaving Fishguard Station on 31 August 1909.

Right: GWR map showing the distances and routes for the Irish sailings across the St George's Channel. Fishguard to Rosslare is shown as 54 nautical miles (nm), Fishguard to Waterford 92 nm, and further south the Cork route is 140 nm, more than twice that of the crossing to Rosslare.

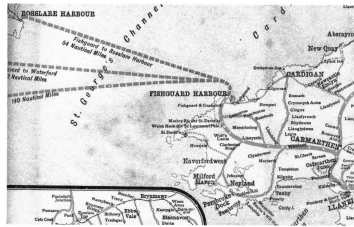

PEMBROKESHIRE

The surface of this county is, generally speaking, composed of easy slopes, but not mountainous, except a ridge of hills which runs from the coast to the border of Carmarthenshire. Pembroke cannot boast of being either a trading or a manufacturing county, though it possesses many facilities for commerce. The South Wales mineral basin terminates here, and becomes shallower as it approaches the extremity. The strata are raised near the surface, and then the quality is impaired.

WHITLAND

Telegraph station at Carmarthen, 13¾ miles.
MONEY ORDER OFFICE at St Clears.

NARBERTH ROAD (For Tenby)

Distance of town from station, 3¾ miles. Telegraph station at Haverfordwest, 11¾ miles, HOTEL – De Rutzen Arms. MARKET DAY – Saturday.
FAIRS – March 21st, May 13th, June 2nd and 29th, August 10th, September 22nd, October 27th, and December 11th.

NARBERTH is a small neat town in the county of Carmarthen, with a population of 1,209. It has the privilege of being represented in Parliament in connection with the borough of Haverfordwest, Fishguard, and St Davids. It has no particular object of attraction, beyond being the best and nearest way by coach from Narberth Road station to the town of

TENBY

POPULATION, 2,982. Telegraph station at New Milford, 13 miles.
HOTELS – White Lion, and Coburg. MARKET DAYS – Wednesday and Saturday.
FAIRS – May 4th Whit Tuesday, July 4th, Oct. 2nd, and Dec. 4th.
RACES in August or September.

Tenby, on the coast of Pembrokeshire, and eleven miles from Pembroke itself, was at a very remote period occupied by the ancient Britons as a fishing town, and is most romantically situated on the eastern and southern sides of a rocky peninsula, stretching out into the Bristol Channel, and rising to the elevation of 100 feet above the level of high water. The houses are well built, and command fine views of the sea; and the beautiful situation of the town, the fine beach, and firm and smooth sands, the transparency of the sea water, and the pleasant walks and extensive drives in the vicinity, have raised it from the decline into which it had for many years previously fallen to a high rank among the most favourite watering-places on the coast. Under the Castle-hill baths, provided with every convenience, are supplied by a capacious reservoir, filled from the sea at every tide. This establishment comprises two spacious pleasure-baths, one for ladies and one for gentlemen, four smaller cold baths, and also a range of warm sea-water and vapour-baths, with apparatus for heating them to any

Milford Haven

Left: Laying the foundation stone for the new Hubberston Dock within the natural harbour of the Milford Haven estuary. From *The Illustrated London News* of 27 August 1864.

Below: Two views of the docks and town. The lower one is from Hakin, which is directly to the west of Milford Haven.

degree of temperature required. The surrounding scenery is extremely beautiful and picturesque. The majestic masses of rock, of various forms and hues, which line the coast; the numerous bays and distant promontories that stretch out into the sea; the receding coast of Carmarthenshire, with the projecting headland of Gower enclosing the great bay of Carmarthen, on the western boundary of which the town is situated; the small islands of Caldey and Lundy, with the distant shores of Somersetshire and Devonshire, combine to impart a high degree of interest and variety to one of the finest marine expanses in the kingdom. On one side of the town there is a drive of eleven miles to the ancient town of Pembroke, through a fine campaign country, studded with churches, villages, and gentlemen's seats, surrounded with plantations and pleasure-grounds, and on the other the country is agreeably diversified with swelling eminences, clothed with verdure, and small valleys richly wooded. The remains of the ancient castle are considerable, though in a very dilapidated condition. A portion of the keep still remains, and the principal gateway, with a square tower and a bastion, are also in a tolerable state of preservation. The ancient walls, which surrounded the town, are still in many places entire. The sands afford delightful promenades, and abound also with shells of varied descriptions, not less than one-half of the British collection of 600 varieties having been found on this coast, among which have been several of value commonly esteemed foreign. The church is a venerable and spacious structure, dating as far back as the year 1250. There is constant steam communication with Bristol.

CLARBESTON ROAD

Distance from station, 3 miles. Telegraph station at Haverfordwest, 5½ miles.
MARKET DAY – Saturday. MONEY ORDER OFFICE at Narberth.

HAVERFORDWEST

POPULATION, 7,019. A telegraph station. HOTEL – Castle.
MARKET DAYS – Tuesday and Saturday. FAIRS – March 20th, April 14th, May 12th, June 12th, July 18th, August 9th, September 4th and 23rd, October 18th, and December 10th.

HAVERFORDWEST is a borough town in Pembrokeshire, South Wales. It stands on a western branch of the river Claddau, which at spring tides is navigable for vessels of a hundred tons burden, and for whose accommodation a number of convenient quays have been erected. The town is built on the steep declivity of a hill, and presents a very picturesque appearance, as the houses rise in terraces one above the other, the whole being crowned by the ruins of the castle. The interior of the town, however, is in many respects inconvenient and disagreeable, as many of the streets are so narrow and steep as almost to prevent horses and carriages from ascending them. But, on the other hand, the spirit of modern improvement has prevailed to a considerable extent, and many new streets and public buildings have been erected. There are three churches, a handsome guild hall, the gaol, and the keep of an ancient castle.

Milford Haven
This is the largest natural harbour in Wales. The first rail links to Milford Haven came with the completion of the South Wales Railway in 1856. At that time, Brunel saw the estuary port at Neyland as a direct link between the railway and the steamships going to New York, and the town grew rapidly as a result.

The hotel is shown above. Milford Haven is still a working port and has a large oil terminal offshore.

Tenby Harbour
Left: Located on the western side of Carmarthan Bay. The railway station opened in 1863. Bradshaw writes at some length on this 'romantically situated' seaside town. *(LoC)*

DISTANCES OF PLACES FROM THE STATION

	Miles		Miles
Abercastle	17¾	Milford	7½
Abernause	17	Pembroke Castle	11½
Benton Castle	9	Penlan Castle	17
Bishop's Palace at St Davids	17¼	Picton Castle	4¾
Cardigan	26	Poyntz Castle	7
Carew Castle	15	Roch Castle	6
Cathedral (St Davids)	16½	Skower and Skokam Islands	12
Cromlech	(2)	Soloa Valley	8
from Nevern Chruch	18	St Bride's Bay	5
Devil's Punch Bowl	20	St Davids	16
Huntersman's Leap	21	Walwin Castle	4

MILFORD ROAD

Telegraph station at Haverfordwest, 4¾ miles.
MONEY ORDER OFFICE at Haverfordwest, 5 miles.

Johnston Hill, in the vicinity, is the seat of Lord Kensington. Anthracite, or smokeless coal, abounds in this district, and it is only wanting to be better known, in order to be generally used in the steamers belonging to the naval and merchant services. It was used by Her Majesty's steam fleet at the review on the 23rd of April, 1856.

It has been proposed to construct a railway, 3½ miles long, from this station to the town of Milford; other modes of conveyance are at present in use.

MILFORD

HOTELS – Royal; Victoria. MARKET DAYS – Tuesday and Saturday.

The town of Milford has a population of 3,007 partially engaged in ship-building. It is pleasantly situated; but since the removal of the royal dockyard and Irish packet station from here, about 1815, to Pater and Pembroke, on the opposite side of the Haven, its importance in a commercial point of view has much declined.

Milford is prettily situated on a sloping point of land, about six miles from the entrance of the Haven, to which it gives its name. Milford haven ought to be viewed from the water. The lower and broadest portion of the Haven runs in an easterly direction for about twelve miles, and then turns abruptly to the north, forming several reaches towards Haverfordwest. The scenery around Milford is very picturesque. On a fork of land, formed by the confluence of the two rivers Cleddy and Cleddau, stands Rose Castle, an ancient seat of the Owens, and higher up on the estuary is Picton Castle.

Brunel's *Great Eastern* steamship

Above: The *Great Eastern* in her prime. Completed in 1859, the ship had been intended for the Australia run, but instead operated out of Milford Haven, sometimes Liverpool, crossing the Atlantic to New York. Following a successful career as a transatlantic cable layer, she was laid up at Milford Haven and offered at auction in October 1885. *Below:* After a period as a floating showboat and advertising hoarding, she was broken up at Rock Ferry on the Mersey in 1889–1890.

Left: Robert Thomas's statue of Brunel on the quayside at Neyland. Erected in 1999, it shows him holding the *Great Eastern* steamship in one hand and a broad gauge loco in the other. It was stolen in 2010, most probably for its value as scrap metal. *(Frank Whittle)*

NEW MILFORD

A telegraph station.

This has become a station of much importance, being the one used for the interchange of traffic to and from the South of Ireland.

PEMBROKE

The capital of the county, and Pater or Pembroke Dock, the seat of a royal dockyard, at the head of that magnificent inlet called Milford Haven, opposite to Neyland station (from which it is distant one and a half mile), and the terminus of the South Wales line, opened in April, 1856. A branch is in progress to unite it with the main line and the beautiful watering place of Tenby; in conjunction with which, and two or three other little boroughs, it returns one member to parliament. Population, 15,071. Both the town and shire take their name from the Welsh words, *Pen fro*, signifying the head of the peninsula, as the town lies on a long point, marked on both sides by a creek or Milford Haven. In this commanding spot, Arnulph de Montgomery began a Norman Castle in 1092, which a few years after was strengthened by the famous Richard de Clare, or Strongbow, before he sailed for the conquest of Ireland. Its ruins still exist on a hill over the town; the round keep is 75 feet high. There is a large cave under the hall; and in one of the town-gates the Earl of Richmond (whose mother was of the Welsh family of Tudor of Tudor, descended from Edward I), afterwards Henry VII, was born. He landed on this part of Wales after his escape from confinement in Brittany; and supported by Rhys ap Thomas, and other Welsh adherents, marched towards Bosworth Field, where his defeat of Richard III, and subsequent marriage with Elizabeth of York, terminated forever the Wars of the Roses.

There is nothing else worth notice in the town, except the old church of St Michael. Two short bridges cross to Monckton (where there was a priory), and to the suburbs on the north side, from whence roads, about two miles long, lead to Pembroke ferry and to the dockyard at *Pater*, which covers a site of 88 acres, fifteen or sixteen of which are occupied by iron building slips. The sea front is nearly half a mile long; one new slip has an open glass and metal roof. Important docks are in progress, which will cost £100,000. The whole is defended by strong forts at Hobb's Point Jetty, formerly the station for the Waterford Mail Packets, now discontinued, near the large hotel. Until 1814 the dockyard was at Milford, five miles to the left, on the north side of the Haven, which has declined since its removal. The establishment of a packet station for New York and the south of Ireland, which is one of the chief objects contemplated by the South Wales Railway Company, may contribute to revive it. It possesses a little coasting trade. *Pill Priory* is near.

On Thorn Island, on the southern side of the entrance into Milford Haven, there are newly-erected fortifications, which are now strongly garrisoned. The noble Haven which it overlooks in in fact the mouth of the Cleddau or Cleddy, and is twelve miles long, by two miles broad, with fifteen bays or creeks in it. As there is plenty of deep water, it would easily hold the entire British navy. At the entrance is St Anne's light. Imogen (one of the sweetest of Shakespeare's heroines), says, in *Cymbeline*, when she receives her husband's letter:

'Oh for a horse with wings! Hear'st thou, Pisanio?
He is at *Milford Haven*. Read and tell me
How far 'tis thither. If one of mean affairs
May plod it in a week, why may not I
Glide thither in a day?
    And, by the way,

Tell me how Wales is made so happy as
To inherit such a haven!'

Here, in 'a mountainous country, with a cave', disguised as a boy, the poor betrayed lady afterwards meets with her royal brothers Guiderus and Arviragus, supposed to be sons of the old shepherd Belarius.

'*Bel*. This youth, howe'er distressed he appears, hath had
Good ancestors.
Arv. How angel like he sings.
Gui. But his neat cookery! He cut our roots in characters;
    And sauc'd our broths, as Juno had been sick,
    And he her dieter.'

In the course of the plot, Lucius, the Roman General lands here:
    After your will have coursed the sea; attending
    You here at Milford Haven, with your ships.

During the troubles of Henry IV's reign, a force of 12,000 French actually landed here to support the rising of Owen Glyndwr.

The peninsula between Milford Haven and the Bristol Channel is bounded by a remarkable broken limestone coast, along which is a succession of the most striking views. When traversed from end to end, it is a walk, from Anglesey, at the Haven's mouth to Tenby, in Carmarthen bay, of twenty or twenty-five miles. Cars may be hired, but, as inns are very rare, it is advisable to take provisions, or you must trust to the chance of shelter at some hospitable farm house. Of these, however, there are but few.

Starting from the old fort near Angle or Nangle Bay, you pass round the east side of the entrance to the Haven, with St Anne's Head and Light on the opposite side, and the island closing up to Bride's Bay, a most enchanting spot, in the distance behind. Rat and Sheep Islands are seen below, the latter near a Danish camp. The broad swell of the Atlantic dashes on the cliffs. At Gupton (seven miles from Angle fort) a little stream comes down to Freshwater Bay, from Castle Martin, an old place, noted for its breed of black hill cattle, and for a cromlech. It had a castle formerly. *Brownslade*, near it, is the seat of J. Mirehouse, Esq. At Linney Head (three miles from Gupton) the finest part of this coast trip commences. 'A greater extent of carboniferous limestone is exposed to view along these shores than in any part of Britain.' – Cliffe's *Book of South Wales.* Keep at the edge of the downs to enjoy it thoroughly. Out in the sea is the Crow rock, a dangerous one, covered at high water. The Castles are two rocks separated from the mainland. Then Flimstone chapel (a ruin); near Bull's Scaughter Bay, another group of stacks or castle rocks, swarming with razorbills, guillemots, kittiwakes, and other sea birds, in a very wild part; another camp near a dark chasm, called the Devil's Cauldron; and then *St Gwan's Head* (seven miles from Linney Head), so called, it is said, after King Arthur's nephew, Sir Gawaine, or Gwain, of old romances. Here the cliffs are 160 or 170 feet high, and the strata in vast horizontal blocks. In a gap, looking down to the sea, is a ruined hermitage, to which you descend by about fifty-three broken steps; it is only 20 feet long. The saint's hiding place in the east wall, and his well are shown, with remnants of past superstition. *Bosherston Meer,* a little further, is a cave, which runs up the land more than quarter of a mile. The roaring of the waves and the wind along this natural tunnel is at times terrific. Before reaching it you pass a remarkable crack in the cliffs, called the Huntsman's Leap. Across Broadhaven Creek (which runs up to Bosheston) to Stackpole Head; then *Stackpole Park*, the modern seat of the Earl of Cawdor, the chief owner of the soil in this quarter. There was a Norman castle of the eleventh century here, built by a baron, whose effigy is in Cheriton church. Fine view from Windmill Hill. Round East Freshwater Bay and Swanslake Bay to *Manorbeer Castle* (eight miles from West Gwan's) close to the shore. It is a fine existing specimen of what a feudal dwelling was in early times. It was built by William de Barri, and was the birth place of Giraldus de Barri (or Cambrensis, i.e., the Welshman); Lord Milford is the present owner. Hence, round Oldcastle Head and Lidstep Point to Giltar Head (fifteen miles from Manor Bay), turning into Carnarvon Bay. Caldy Island and its lighthouse about two miles off. About twenty miles to the E.S.E., if the weather is favourable, you may catch sight of the Worm's Head, on the other side of the bay, a most striking object. Caldy has a chapel and remains of a priory upon it, incorporated with the seat of a gentleman who is lord of the island. At *Penally*, a pretty chapel and old cross; shells and seaweeds on the shore. Old castle at Trellowyn, and mineral springs at Gumperton. Then Tenby (two or three miles from Giltar Point), a most delightful bathing place to stop at.

Up the *Cleddy* are *Lawrenny Hall*, seat of L. Phillipps, Esq., on a bold point where two creeks branch off, one to Carew, Landshipping Quay, near which the two Cleddys unite. The west Cleddy may be followed to *Boulston*, an old seat of the Wogans; and Haverfordwest. The east Cleddy, to *Picton*, Lord Milford's seat – a well wooded park, with an old Norman castle; and *Slebech*, the seat of the Baron de Rutzen. Here is an old church of the Knights Templars.

In the neighbourhood of Pembroke are the following: *Upton Castle*, seat of Rev. W. Evans, *Lamphey Court* (two miles), belongs to C. Mathias, Esq., and is

Ocean Express at Fishguard
Above: Carriages of the Ocean Express at Fishguard Station. These special trains were operated by the GWR between 1908 and 1914, and only when liners were calling at the harbour.

Left: Postcard showing the lavish interior of the Dining Saloon.

Below: Brochure showing the Cunard Line route map.

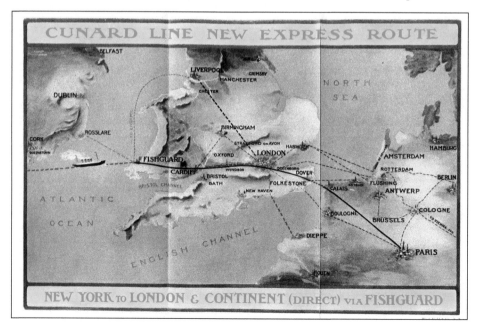

close to the fine ruins of a deserted palace of the bishops of St Davids, in a rich Gothic style; the great hall is 76 feet long. There is another by the same builder (Bishop Gower), at the city of St Davids, the see of which, now much despoiled, had at one time six different residences for its prelates. Its cathedral, which is cruciform, 200 feet by 120 feet, with fine tower, 127 feet, is being restored, and contains the shrine visited by Henry I and Edward I, the road to which (16 miles from Haverfordwest) is the most execrable in the United Kingdom, but replete with scenery magnificently grand. *Carew* (four miles), is another of those old baronial seats so abundant in South Wales; it was built in Henry I's reign, by the ancestor of the Fitzgeralds. There are two great halls 100 feet and 80 feet long. Effigies in the church; and an old roadside cross, 14 feet high. *Orielton* (6 miles) belongs to the Owens.

There has been a Steam Packet communication opened out between this place and Ireland, of which the traveller, if he think fit, might avail himself.

On the last day of August 1909, Cunard's *Mauretania* called at Fishguard on her way to Liverpool. This gave the opportunity to drop the mails from the USA so that they would reach London much more quickly, but it also ensured that those passengers for the south of England could be at their destinations much more quickly too. Mail workers are shown, above, loading the mail onto the SS *Smeaton*, which operated from the harbour from 1909 to 1910.

Pontypridd

At one time Pontypridd boasted of having the longest station platform in the world. The photograph *above* shows fodder being collected for the pit ponies during the 1910 coal strike. *(LoC) Below:* Postcard image of the 1911 train crash near Pontypridd. Eleven people were killed in a collision between a passenger train and a coal train on the Taff Vale line.

TRAIN DISASTER Nr PONTYPRIDD. 23-1-11.

South Wales Branch Lines

Monmouthshire Line

The Eastern and Western Valleys Lines turn off at this point to the right, passing through districts rich in mineral products, but not of essential importance to the general tourist. The stations on the Western Line are BASSALLEG JUNCTION, TYDEE, RISCA, CROSS KEYS, CHAPEL BRIDGE, ABERCARNE, NEW BRIDGE, CRUMLIN, LLANHILLETH, ABERBEEG, CWM, VICTORIA, EBBW VALE, ABERTILLERY, and BLAINA. Those on the eastern Branch, LLANTANAM, CWMBRAN, PONTNEWYDD, PONTRHYDYRUN, PONTPOOL, PONTNEWYNNYDD, ABERSYCHAN, CWM AVON, and BLAENAVON.

Returning to Newport we now proceed by the

WEST MIDLAND

Newport to Abergavenny and Hereford.

In ten minutes after leaving Newport we reach PONTNEWYDD, and in ten minutes more, the station

PONTYPOOL ROAD

Distance from the town of the same name, 1 mile. A telegraph station.

Near is *Pontypool Park*, Hanbury Leigh Esq. This forms the junction with the

Taff Vale Extension

A short line, 16 miles long, running into the Taff Vale Line at Quaker's Yard. The stations on the line are PONTYPOOL, CRUMLIN, TREDEGAR, RHYMNEY JUNCTION, LLANCAICH, and QUAKER'S YARD.

COLEFORD, MONMOUTH, USK, AND PONTYPOOL

Pontypool Road to Monmouth.

About a mile and a half beyond Pontypool Road this line turns off; and at the distance of about 3½ miles further, we cross the river at Usk, and stop at the station of that name.

Two bridges over the River Monnow at Monmouth: *Above*, a print dated 1799 of the old Tibbs footbridge with St Mary's church in the background. *Below*, a photograph of the fortified medieval gateway of the Monnow Bridge from around 1890. *(LoC)*

USK

The town is situated a little to the right of the station, and is a place of great antiquity. Considerable remains of a castle where Richard III and Edward IV are reputed to have been born, are to be seen; likewise part of a priory. Fine salmon fishing.

Llangibby Castle (3 miles).

Passing LLANDENNY Station, we arrive at

RAGLAN ROAD,

Which is available for foot passengers only.

Here are the fine remains of the castle built by Sir W. Thomas in the 14th century. The Marquis of Worcester defended it for four years against the Parliament: it is now a most picturesque ruin. It gives title of Baron Raglan to a descendant – the late Lord Fitzroy Somerset, Commander-in-Chief in the late war in the Crimea. He was military secretary to Wellington, and lost an arm at Waterloo. What it was in the 16th century we may hear from the poet Churchyard; he speaks of it as –

A castle fine that Raglan hight – stands moted almost round,
Made of freestone, upright, straight as line,
Whose workmanship in Beauty doth abound.

DINGESTOW

Or Dynstow. In a barn, among beautiful orchards, may be seen the remains of Grace Dieu Abbey.

MONMOUTH

Telegraph station at Pontypool road, 18 miles.
HOTELS – Beaufort Arms; King's Head.

MONMOUTH, the capital of Monmouthshire, is on a delightful part of the Wye, at the junction of the Monnow, a parliamentary borough, returning one member, conjointly with Newport and Usk, with an agricultural population of 5,710, which is rather on the decrease; but this will no doubt be augmented by the recent opening of the railway from Pontypool. It was the ancient Blestium, from which a Roman road, in the direction of the present one, went to Usk. There was a castle here, even in Saxon times, which afterwards became the residence of Henry IV, and here, in 1387, his famous son Henry V was born – 'Harry of Monmouth' – the immortal Prince Hal of Shakespeare.

The few remains of this castle (which belongs to the Duke of Beaufort), stand among houses on a ridge over the Monnow, to the west near the gaol, the walls being 6 to 10 feet thick. Here is shown the room in which Henry was born, and the great hall by the side of it. There is a statue of him in the Market Place.

Within a short distance of the town are the following objects of notice: The *Wye*, so celebrated for its uniform breadth, lofty cliffs, winding course, and picturesque

Right: In 1930 this elephant, known as Lossey, was photographed having a splash about in the River Monnow at Monmouth. The local newspaper reported that she had escaped from the Mop Fair in the town. *(Andrew Helme)*

Above: The statue to the pioneer motorist and aviator Charles Rolls stands in front of the Shire Hall in Agincourt Square, Monmouth. Rolls was killed during a flying display held at Bournemouth in 1910. His family, significant landowners in the Monmouth area, had the statue erected in his memory.

Left: Postcard view of Crane Street in Pontypool, *c.* 1905.

scenery, which is perpetually changing its character. Elegant and commodious boats are kept here for the use of tourists. 'The stranger cannot do better than hire Samuel Dew, whom he will find by Monmouth Bridge. Sam is one of the steadiest and cleverest of Wye watermen, knows the river well, and is quite used to guiding those who are in search of the beautiful.' – *The Land we Live in.*

Near the junction of the Trothey, about a mile from Monmouth, is *Troy House*, an old seat of the Duke of Beaufort, with old portraits and gardens, where the Marquis of Worcester gave Charles I a dish of fruit 'from Troy.' 'Truly my lord,' said the king, 'I have heard that corn grows where Troy stood, but I never thought that there had grown apricots there before.' Here is Henry's cradle (so called), and the armour he wore at Agincourt. About 6 miles down the Wye is Beacon Hill, 1,000 feet high, near Trelech Cross (three Druid stones), and below that Landogo Bigswear, Tintern Abbey, Wyndcliffe, Chepstow (17 miles by water); *Wonastow*, seat of Sir W. Pilkington, baronet, is a very old seat, which belonged to the Herberts. *Treowen*, near it, is another, but now turned into a farm house. Up the Trothey is *Llantillio House.*

A pretty road leads to Beaulieu Grove on the top, near the handsome spire church of Lantillio Crossenny, and the ruins of White Castle, a fortress built by the early Norman possessors of this county. In ascending the beautiful valley of the Monnow, there are two other castles worth notice – Skenfrith and Grosmont – the latter being under Greig Hill, near a small cross church. Most of these structures were formerly part of the Duchy of Lancaster, through John of Gaunt, but now belong, with large possessions, to the Beaufort family. From Monmouth, up the Wye, you pass Dixton Church, a pretty rustic building; then New Weir, Symond's Yat, Courtfield (where Henry V was nursed), &c, till you come to Ross. But the best plan is to descend from that place (see the *Wye*).

An excursion may be made to the *Forest of Dean*, and its interesting scenery. You pass (taking the Coleford Road) the Buckstone, an immense Logan stone, on a hill, 56 feet round at the top, and tapering off to 3 at the bottom. Coleford Church is modern, the old one having been destroyed in the civil wars, when Lord Herbert routed some of the parliament people here. About 3 miles north-east is the Speech House, where the miners hold their meetings. To the south, in the direction of Offa's Dyke, which may still be traced, is *Clearwell Park*, the seat of the dowager Countess of Dunraven, where a great heap of Roman money was found in 1847, and St Briaval's, with its *May Pole* and hundred court, part of a Norman castle. There are many deserted mines. The wood is cut for hoops, poles, and other purposes.

A good stone bridge across the Wye, and one the Monnow – an ancient stone building, called the Welsh Gate, with a Norman chapel (St Thomas's) at the foot. Many of the houses are white-washed, and, as they are dispersed among gardens and orchards, the view of the town in summer is picturesque. The parish church of *St Mary* has a tapering spire 200 feet. It was attached to a priory, of which there are remains in a private house adjoining. The handsome oriel window is called the 'study' of Geoffrey of Monmouth, but he was born in the 11th century, long before such a style was invented. He was a Welsh monk (Geoffrey ap Arthur), who turned the British Chronicles, fables and all, into rugged Latin. To

Abergavenny

Above: A Photochrom image looking across Abergavenny to Holy Mountain, *c.* 1890. *(LoC)*

Below: A surprisingly quiet Frogmore Street in the middle of the town.

him, however, we are indebted for Shakespeare's *King Lear*, and the Sabrina of Milton's *Comus*.

Monmouth was once famous for its woollen caps, 'the most ancient, general, warm, and profitable covering for men's heads on this island,' according to Fuller. The manufacture was afterwards transferred to Bewdley. This is, or was, a capper's chapel in the church, 'better carved and gilded than any other part of it.' Fletcher takes care to remember this.

The well-endowed free school was founded by W. Jones, who, from a poor shop-boy at this place, became a rich London merchant. Newland was his birth-place; and there, after quitting London, he showed himself under the disguise of poverty, but being told to try for relief at Monmouth, where he had been at service, he repaired hither, was kindly received, and then revealed who he was.

One of the walks is at Chippenham meadow, near the junction of the Monnow and Wye, under a grove of elms. Anchor and May Hills are good points of view. Past may Hill (across the Wye) is *Kymin Hill*, the east half of which is Gloucestershire.

West Midland Main Line

Pontypool Road to Abergavenny

Passing the station of NANTYDERRY, or Goitre, we arrive at PENPERGWM, near which is *Llanover*, the seat of Lord Llanover, and three miles to the right is *Clytha*. Proceeding along the valley of the USK, we soon arrive at:

ABERGAVENNY

A telegraph station. HOTEL – Angel. MARKET DAY – Tuesday.
FAIRS – Third Tuesday in March, May 14th, June 24th (wool), Tuesday before July 20th, September 25th, and November 19th. RACES in April.

This interesting old place, of 4,621 inhabitants, stands among the Monmouthshire Hills, near the Sugar Loaf, Blorenge, and other peaks, in a fine part of Usk, where the Gavenny joins it, and gives name to the town, which the Romans, who had a station here, called Gobannium. It was formerly noted for its old castle and springs, founded by Hammeline de Balun at the Conquest, the former for the purpose of guarding the pass into Wales. This feudal structure afterwards came to the Nevilles, who still take title from it. A Tudor gate, from which there is a fine prospect, is the chief remain. Later still Abergavenny became celebrated for its Welsh wigs, made of goats' hair, some of which sold at 40 guineas each. Physicians also used to send patients here to drink goats' whey. But its present prosperity arises from its flannel weaving, and the valuable coal and iron works at Clydach, Blaenavon, &c., in the neighbourhood – a state of things likely to be much increased by the Newport, Abergavenny and Hereford Railway, part of the important chain which unites South Wales to Liverpool and the north of England.

The old bridge of 15 arches crosses the Usk. The church has some ancient tombs of the Beauchamps, and other possessors of the lordship. Traces of the old priory exist

BRITISH COAL STRIKE - LLWYNPIA, SOUTH WALES, A COLLIERY VILLAGE

The coalfields of South Wales fuelled Britain's industrial might throughout the nineteenth century and continued in production well into the twentieth. *Above:* Miners at a Monmouthshire colliery. *Left:* Mining communities were built cheek by jowl with the mines. *(LoC)*

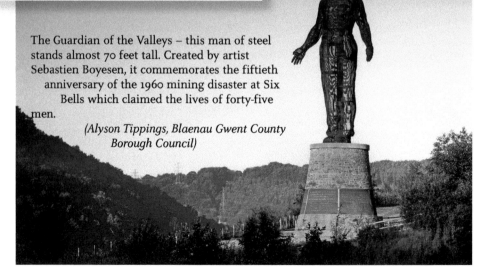

The Guardian of the Valleys – this man of steel stands almost 70 feet tall. Created by artist Sebastien Boyesen, it commemorates the fiftieth anniversary of the 1960 mining disaster at Six Bells which claimed the lives of forty-five men.

(Alyson Tippings, Blaenau Gwent County Borough Council)

near it. There is also an old grammer school, and a modern Cymreidiggion Society's Hall for Welsh bardic meetings – Monmouth being essentially Welsh, though separated from the principality since Henry VIII's time. Antiquaries say that until feudal tenures were abolished by Charles II, Abergavenny castle used to give its holders their title by mere possession – like Arundel Castle, in Sussex, instead of by writ or by patent.

The views from the Sugar Loaf, which is 1,856 feet high, are magnificent. It takes three hours to ascend it. A still more beautiful prospect is enjoyed from St Michael's old Chapel on Skyrrid Vawr. The White Castle is near the mountain. Raglan Castle, which the famous Marquis of Worcester held out so stoutly against Cromwell, is also near (8 miles), on the Monmouth Road. Its machicolated gate, hall, chapel, the yellow tower, etc., are in excellent preservation, through the care of its owner, the Duke of Beaufort. Llanthony Abbey stands in a wild part of the Rhonda. The scenery of the Usk, from Abergavenny up to Brecon, is very romantic, as it winds round the black mountains, in one of the highest peaks of which it rises above Trecastle. Excellent trout fishing.

The Merthyr, Tredegar, and Abergavenny Railway runs out to the left at this place, and will, when finished, prove to be a very valuable link in the railway system, as there will be direct communication between the more westerly districts of South Wales and those of the Midland Counties. That part of the line open at present passes through GOVILAN and GILWERNB to BRYNMAWR. The rest of the journey through Tredegar to Merthyr is performed by coach, which runs once a day each way, in connection with one of the trains.

LLANFIHANGEL and PANDY stations.

PONTRILAS
Telegraph station at Hereford, 10¾ miles.
MONEY ORDER OFFICE at Hereford.

Below: Completed in 1857, the Crumlin Viaduct carried the Taff Vale Extension of the Newport, Abergavenny & Hereford Railway over the River Ebbw.

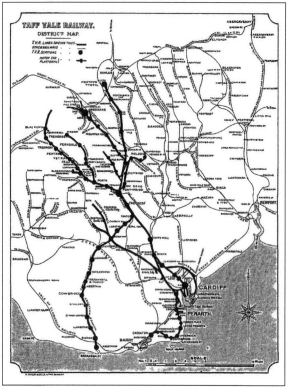

The Taff Vale Railway

This is one of the oldest and best known railways of South Wales. Its primary function was to connect the many coalfields and foundries in the valleys with the docks at Cardiff. Started in 1836, the main section between Merthyr and Cardiff was completed in 1841. The TVR operated as an independent railway until 1922 when it became a part of the GWR. It was a busy line and at its peak two trains passed through Pontypridd every minute. The railway company held a virtual monopoly over the Rhondda's mine and foundry owners until the construction of the Barry Railway in the 1880s. The Taff Vale line is still in use.

Left: The gentle curve of the Cefn Coed Viaduct, just to the north of Merthyr Tydfil. The third longest viaduct in Wales, it was built in 1866 to carry the Brecon & Merthyr railway over the River Taff at Pontycapel. *(Perceval)*

ST DEVERAUX and TRAM INN stations passed, we arrive at Hereford.

[Branch from Cardiff on the Taff Vale to Merthyr and Brecon]

TAFF VALE

Cardiff to Aberdare and Merthyr.

LLANDAFF
POPULATION, 6,585. Telegraph station at Cardiff, 3½ miles.
HOTEL – Railway. MONEY ORDER OFFICE at Cardiff.

LLANDAFF, a small decayed village, but the seat of a diocese, founded in the 5th century, having a half ruined *Cathedral*, 270 feet long, chiefly in the early English style. The south door is Norman. Some old monuments are seen – one being ascribed to Dubritias, the first bishop.

From Llandaff, in the course of about half an hour, we are hurried past the stations of WALNUT TREE Junction, TREFOREST, and NEWBRIDGE, the junction of the Rhondda Valley line, via PORTH to YSTRAD and TREHERBERT. ABERDARE BRANCH.

MOUNTAIN ASH and TREAMAN stations.

ABERDARE
POPULATION, 32,299. A telegraph station. HOTELS – Boot and railway.
MARKET DAY – Saturday. FAIRS – April 1st and 16th, November 13th.

The scenery of the vale of Cynon here is charming. A little beyond there is a junction with the Vale of Neath Railway to Merthyr.

Taff Vale Main Line continued.

QUAKER'S YARD and TROEDYRHIEW stations.

MERTHYR
POPULATION, 83,875. A telegraph station. HOTELS – Castle, Bush.
MARKET DAYS – Wednesday and Saturday.
BANKERS – Wilkins and Co.; Branch of West of England and South Wales District Banking Company.

MERTHYR TYDVIL is a parliamentary borough, the great mining town, in South Wales, 21 miles from Cardiff, with which there is a railway communication by a branch out of the South Wales line. It stands up the Taff, among the rugged and

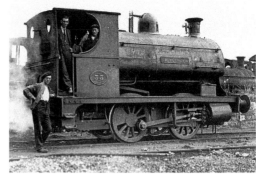

Dowlais Ironworks and Steelworks

Bradshaw writes at some length about the foundry at Dowlais. 'Visitors should see the furnaces by night when the red glare of the flames produces an uncommonly striking effect.' Founded in 1759, from the mid-nineteenth century it was run by Lady Charlotte Guest and Edward Divett following the death of Thomas Guest. The pair revived the company through the adoption of the Bessemer process for steel production. Lady Guest died in 1895. Her daughter-in-law's name is commemorated in works loco No. 33, *Lady Cornelia*. The main works survived until the 1930s, ceasing production at Dowlais in 1936.

Below: Brecon & Merthyr Junction Railway locomotive No. 1 *Merthyr Cefn Coed*, photographed on the Cyfartha private line.

barren-looking hills in the north-east corner of Glamorganshire, the richest county in Wales for mineral wealth. About a century ago the first iron works were established here, since which the extension has been amazingly rapid. Blast furnaces, forges, and rolling mills are scattered on all sides. Each iron furnace is about 55 feet high, containing 5,000 cubic feet; and capable of smelting 100 tons of pig-iron weekly, as there are upwards of 50, the annual quantity of metal may be tolerably estimated; but great as the supply may seem, it is scarcely equal to the demand created for it by railways. The largest works are those belonging to Lady Guest and Messers. Crawshay, where 3,000 to 5,000 hands are employed. At Guest's Dowlais works there are 18 or 20 blast furnaces, besides many furnaces for puddling, balling, and refining; and 1,000 tons of coal a day are consumed.

Visitors should see the furnaces by night when the red glare of the flames produces an uncommonly striking effect. Indeed, the town is best visited at that time, for by day it will be found dirty, and irregularly built, without order or management, decent roads or footpaths, no supply of water, and no public building of the least note, except Barracks, and a vast Poor-House, lately finished, in the shape of a cross, on heaps of the rubbish accumulated from the pits and works. Cholera and fever are, of course, at home here, in scenes which would shock even the most 'eminent defender of the filth,' and which imperatively demand that their Lady owner should become one of 'the Nightingale sisterhood' for a brief space of time. Out of 695 couples married in 1845, 1,016 persons signed with marks, one great secret of which social drawback is the unexampled rapidity with which the town has sprung up; but we hope that proper measures will be taken henceforth by those who draw enormous wealth from working these works, to improve the condition of the people. Coal and iron are found together in this part of Wales, the coal being worked mostly by levels, in beds 2 to 3 feet thick. Besides the large and small works in and about Merthyr, there are those at Aberdare (a growing rival to Merthyr), Herwain, Pentwain, Blaenavon, Brynmawr, Nantyglo, Ebbew (w as oo) Vale, Beaufort, Tredegar, Rhimney, Sirhowy, etc., nearly all seated at the head of the valleys, and many of them being in the neighbouring county of Monmouth, which, though reckoned part of England, is essentially Welsh in its minerals, scenery, and people. Railways and canals now traverse these valleys to the sea.

Merthyr Tydvil, as well as its church, derives its name, signifying the Martyr Tydvil, from St Tudfyl, the daughter of Brysham (a Welsh chief) who was put to death for her religion in the early ages of the British church. Many such confessors are commemorated in the designation bestowed on parishes in Wales.

In the neighbourhood are the following objects of notice. The Taff may be ascended to Quaker's Yard and Newbridge, where there are large metal works, and a bridge, called Pont-y-Prid in Welsh, remarkable as the production of a self-taught local architect, named Edwards, who built it in 1751. It is a single arch, with a rise of one-fourth of the span, which is 140 feet, yet it is only 2½ feet thick in the crown. Once and twice it fell when completed, but the third time the builder was successful, experience having taught him to diminish the strain from its own weight, by boring three large holes on each side near the piers. Following the Neath rail, you come to

Pont-neath-Vaughan, at the head of the fine Vale of Neath, within a few miles of which are the Hefeste, Purthin, and its branches, which are 40 to 70 or 80 feet down. One on the Mellte is particularly worth notice, as it flows for half-a-mile through a limestone cave, and then re-appears just before it sweeps down a fall of 40 feet, with so clean a curve that people have actually taken shelter from the rain under it, on a narrow ledge in the face of the rock. The smaller spouts are called Sewbs (*w* as *oo*). These are all in Brecknockshire; but there is one of 90 feet at Merlin Court, half-way down the Vale of Neath; and to the right of this an ancient Roman way, called Sarn Helen, or via Julia Montana, may yet be traced. It went from an important Roman station. The direct road from Merthyr to Brecon is through a lofty pass, called Glyn Tarrell, having the Brecnockshire Beacons, 2,862 feet high on one side, and Mount Cafellente, 2,394 feet high, on the other. A considerable portion of this route has been laid with rails, and with the exception of a small portion from Merthyr to Dowlais, which is at present performed by coach, is in operation.

The route lies through DOWLAIS, DOLYGAER, TALYBONT, and TALLYLLYN to

BRECON

Telegraph station at Abergavenny, 21 miles. HOTELS – The Castle; Swan.

MARKET DAYS – Wednesdays and Saturdays.

FAIRS – First Wednesday in March, July 5, September 9, November 16; also in March and November 16, for hiring. RACES in September.

This place is situated in the midst of very beautiful mountain scenery, has a population of 5,673, returning one member to parliament. It is 20 miles from Abergavenny, and communicable by coach every day. The principle buildings consist of three churches, County Hall, and Market House, very handsome new Assize Courts, built in 1843, Barracks, Theatre, Infirmary, a bridge of seven arches over the USK, from which is a fine view; there are also an Independent Training College and Grammar School at which Jones, the county historian, was educated.

Here are the remains of an old castle, consisting of the 'Ely Tower', so called from Dr Morton, Bishop of Ely, who was a prisoner at the instance of Richard III, and as the scene of the conference between the Bishop and the Duke of Buckingham. Newmarch, a Norman baron, was the founder of the castle. Hugh Price, the founder of Jesus College, at Oxford, was born here; and Shakespeare's Fluellen, or Sir David Gow lived in the neighbourhood. He was knighted at Agincourt by Henry V, when at the point of death, having sacrificed his own life to save the king's. Another native of the Brecon was Mrs Siddons. The 'Shoulder of Mutton' Inn is pointed out as the place of her nativity. It stands in a romantic part of the Usk, by the banks of which beautiful walks are laid out. To the north of it (22 miles by the lower and 17 by the upper road) is Builth. There are good sulphur springs in this quarter, viz: Park Wells, Llanwrtyd Wells, Llandrindod Wells, &c. Making the descent of the Usk you come to Crickhowell, where there is good angling, and (what is rare in the county) a spire church.

Central Wales

Although a continuous line from Oswestry, the title of the company here takes that of the ...

OSWESTRY AND NEWTOWN

Running through the stations of LLYNCLYS, PANT, LLANYMYNECH (the junction of a short line, via LLANSINFFEAID to LLANFYLLIN, a place celebrated for its ponies), FOUR CROSSES, ARDDLEEN, POOL QUAY, and BUTTINGTON, to WELSHPOOL; but, should time permit, we recommend the tourist to leave the road at Oswestry, and pass by the vale of Tanat for its beautiful scenery, Llangynog, and old cell of St Melangel, near it, to Llanfyllin, thence by Guilsfield Church (at Carvn, close by a Roman camp and road) to

WELSHPOOL
A place of considerable trade, in flannels, and in malt. Population, 7,304. The Severn here becomes navigable. About 1 mile from the town is Powis Castle, the ancient seat of the Clive family, occupying a commanding situation; it overlooks a vast tract of country, and is a large and magnificent seat 8 miles north-west is Llanfawr. On the hill above is the site of the old Roman station Castell Caer Einion. The River Vyrnwy, here is a good angling stream, indeed the whole of the streams, and the Linns (of which there are several) abound with fish, and on every hill there are the remains of camps or entrenchments.

FORDEN station.

MONTGOMERY
Population, 1,276.

At this place are the remains of two castles, and an immense camp with four ditches to be seen. The church is cruciform, and contains some interesting monuments.

Making for the banks of the Severn, we come to the pretty little village of ABERMULE, (the junction of a short line to Kerry) situated at the junction of the rivers Mule and Severn, a little to the left of which is Castell Dolforgan an old ruin on a hill – but surrounded by beautiful scenery. About four miles beyond is the busy little town of

NEWTOWN
Population, 5,916.

There is an old church here, some of the ornaments of which were spoil from the Abbey Cwinhir, in Radnorshire. A spacious flannel hall has been erected.

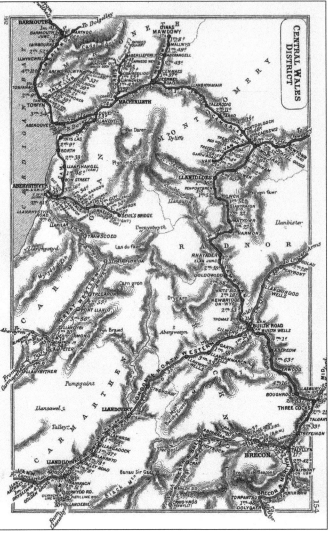

Above: Barmouth's long wooden viaduct across the River Mawddach was completed in 1867, three years after the publication of Bradshaw's guide.

Cambrian Railways

From 1864 onwards, the numerous railways of central Wales were incorporated within the CR, later absorbed into the GWR. Today, the Cambrian Heritage Railway operates trains on the Llynclys South to Pant line.

A short distance beyond Newtown is a romantic glen and waterfall; we then come to Llan-yr-Afange (the Beaver's pool) and four remarkable camps.

Passing the station of SCAFELL, we next come to that of MOAT LANE, the junction of the line called the

NEWTOWN AND MACHYNLLETH

Leaving the station westward we soon come to the small hamlet of CAERSWS, which has the remains of two Roman camps. The river Carno falls into the Severn at this point. We then leave the latter, and taking a direction parallel with the former, come to the town of

CARNO, remarkable for the bloody contentions which, in the earlier history of the principality, from time to time took place amongst its princes.

LLANBYNMAIR AND CLIMES ROAD are respectively passed and our arrival announced at ...

MACHYNLLETH

Supposed to be the Roman Maglona. Here Owen Glyndwr assembled his parliament on being chosen Prince of Wales. The neighbourhood is full of objects of antiquity. At a distance of 11 miles to the west we come to the town of

TOWYN, a thoroughly Welsh town, and a most rural watering place. St Cadfan's Church will delight an antiquarian. Hence follow the mountain road, by the majestic Cader Idris, whose Cyclopean precipices are upheaved in our very path, to

DOLGELLEY. Here it will be found necessary to have a guide for its exploration, unless you have an ordnance map. Nearly 3,000 feet high, its summit commands a most extensive panoramic view, with Snowdon on one side, Wrekin on another, Pilnlimmon to the south, and the Brecknockshire Beacons beyond. Dolgelley itself is a lovely place, and may be made the centre of many an interesting excursion.

The beautiful ruins of Cymner Abbey; Nannau Park, the scene of the deadly feud between Howel Sele and Glyndwr; the Waterfalls; the Vale of Mawddach; the Precipice walk around Moel-Cynwch; the Torrent Walk, the property of the Caerynwych family, and the Abergwynant Walks, the property of Sir Henry Banbury; and the watering place of

BARMOUTH may be visited from this. 10 miles up the coast from Barmonth is Harlech, with its historical old ruined castle, from which Craig Ddrwg and the Rhinog Faur (upwards of 2,000 feet high) may be climbed, with every yard full of Druidical and British remains.

ABERYSTWITH, on the coast of Cardiganshire, situated on a bold eminence, overhanging the sea, at the junction of the Ystwith and the Rhydol. The castle – its chief lion – was built by Gilbert de Strongbow, in the reign of Henry I, and now a mere ruin, is throned upon a projection of slate rock, protecting the town on

Wales is blessed with a number of preserved heritage railways, mostly narrow gauge. *Above:* Welshpool & Llanfair Light Railway No. 2 *Countess* at Raven Square, Welshpool. *(Peterjhw07) Left:* Ruston diesel loco at the Corris Craft Centre in Machynlleth in 1992. *(Gillet's Crossing) Below:* W&LLR No. 14 at Castle Caereinion. *(fairlightworks)*

the sea side, while on the other it commands the entire estuary of the two rivers, meeting at their point of confluence. Northward of the castle is a level beach, some hundred yards in length, to which succeeds a long range of slate rocks, worn into caverns and recesses by the dashing of the waves. Among the ruins is the favourite promenade, which, from its elevation, commands a magnificent view of the whole line of coast that forms Cardigan Bay. Nearly in the middle of this bay Aberystwith is seated, whence may be seen to the north a long irregular line, formed at first by the projecting coast of Merioneth, and then continued out to sea by the long mountainous promontory of Carnarvon, terminated by the Isle of Bardsey. There is no station southward of Carnarvonshire from which the Welsh Alps may be so advantageously seen as from Aberystwith Castle, or some of the surrounding cliffs. The lofty hills which bound the estuary of the Dovey, and raise their broad backs far above the Cardigan rocks, are surmounted by Cader Idris and its subject cliffs. These are overtopped by the giant mountains of Carnarvonshire, among which, in clear weather, the sharp peak of Snowdon itself may be discerned preeminent above the neighbouring crags. This wide expanse of water, diversified by numerous steamers and vessels in every direction – some steering out for different ports in the bay, some further out at sea, and slowly shaping their course for Liverpool, Bristol, or Irish havens, while others, almost stationary, are busily employed in fishing – affords a varied and pleasant panorama of marine scenery. Pont ar Fynach, or the Devil's Bridge, is not more than 12 miles distant. A small portion of the Aberystwith and Welsh Coast Railway beyond Machynlleth is now open. It extends through GLYN-DOVEY and YNYS-LAS to BORTH, on the coast of Cardigan about 8 miles short of Aberystwith.

Returning again to the station at Moat Lane, we pursue our course via LLANDINAM and DOLWEN to

LLANIDLOES

Situated at the confluence of the rivers Clywedog and Severn, returns one member to parliament, and has a population of 3,127, principally engaged in the manufacture of woollen and coarse flannels. The church contains some interesting remains. From this we may visit the source of the Rheidol, and Blaen Hafran, the source of the Severn on the edge of Plinlimmon. The road hence to Machynlleth is full of grand scenery (a distance of 18 miles), and we may add, the wildest road in the kingdom. On the completion of the lines of railway from Llanidloes to Llandovery and the south, the whole of central Wales, abounding in rugged defiles, in secluded glens, darksome rivers (but full of fish), the sources of the Severn and the Wye, and many a relic of our stalwart ancestors, will be opened up to the tourist.

Great Western continued

Proceeding onwards from Gobowen, with St Martin's 1 mile on the right, and Selattyn 1 mile to the left, we soon come to the Chirk Viaduct, which carries us across the lovely vale of Ceiriog, and into the Welsh county of Denbigh, and stop at Chirk.

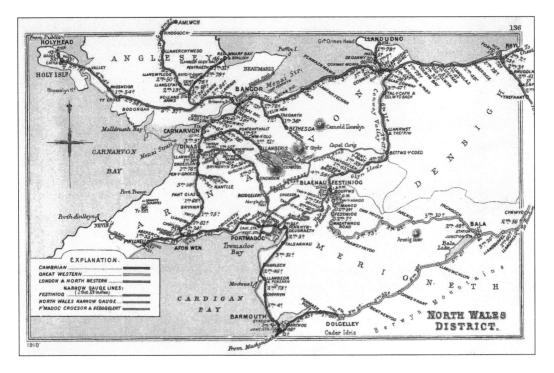

This diagram of the railways in North Wales, *c.* 1905, shows the Cambrian Railway reaching up from Barmouth and around the top of Cardigan Bay, the yellow of the GWR reaching as far as Festiniog, and the LNWR along the northern coast to Bangor and crossing the Menai Straits to connect with the boats at Holyhead. The narrow gauge lines into the mountains are represented by the North Wales, the Festiniog and the Portmadoc, Croesser & Beddgelert. Mount Snowdon is shown more or less in the centre of the diagram.

Above: Side by side, the viaduct and aqueduct which straddle the Ceirog valley near Chirk. The taller railway viaduct of 1848 was built for the Shrewsbury to Chester Railway, while the 1801 aqueduct, designed by Thomas Telford, carries the Llangollen Canal.

North Wales and Anglesey

CHIRK

HOTEL – Castle Arms.

Pleasantly situated on the brow of a hill, surrounded by fertile meadows and wooded banks. The neighbourhood affords various rural entertainments for tourists and visitors. Chirk Viaduct is considered a beautiful engineering gem, and viewed from a hill on the south-west side of the valley, near Pont Feun, is seen to great advantage, and discloses through its arches the lovely vale of Ceiriog.

Parallel with the Chirk Viaduct is the aqueduct, built by Telford, which conveys the Ellesmere canal over the vale of Ceiriog.

In 1164, here took place the most sanguinary battle ever fought between the English and Welsh. Many of the English slain were buried in Offa's Dyke nearby, which still goes by the name of the Pass of Graves.

Overlooking the village is the remarkably interesting and ancient mansion called *Chirk Castle*, the seat of R. Myddelton Biddulph, Esq. This noble looking edifice has been preserved from ruin, and may be regarded as a perfect model of the 'time-honoured castles of the ancient lords of the soil'. From its summit the prospect is not only extensive, but grand, overlooking seventeen counties.

A short distance further on to the left is Bryn-kinailt, the residence of Lord Dungannon, of the Trevor family. The Iron Duke's mother belonged to this family, and here the illustrious warrior passed a great portion of his boyhood; and beyond, in the same direction is the Quinta, the seat of Thos. Barnes, Esq.

The *Great Dee Viaduct*. Crossing the Dee at one of the loveliest spots in the principality of Wales, where nature has grouped the various elements of beauty in the richest profusion, and art has recorded its triumphs by first-class works, the view from the top of the viaduct, for extent and beauty, is unequalled. Beneath winds the Dee, from which rise the Eglwyseg Rocks with serrated outline on the left bank, while the mountains forming the continuation of the Berwyn range abut on the right bank; their lower slopes are richly cultivated, and on successive terraces are dotted the white cottages of the Welsh peasantry, while masses of dark wood crown the projecting heights.

The aqueduct of *Pont-y-Cysylltan*, is seen as you cross about a mile distant front the viaduct, and forms a striking-feature in the prospect. This stupendous viaduct consists of nineteen semi-circular arches of 60-feet span and the height from the bed of the river to the top of the parapet at the centre pier is 148 feet. Its length is 1,532 feet. The viaduct is founded on the solid rock, and is built of stone, with the exception of the interior arching, which is of hard fire bricks. The grain of the stone is beautiful, and the work is so built as to convey to the mind the idea of great strength and solidity. This work of art occupied Telford ten years in its construction.

Bridging the Dee

Flowing from Snowdonia eastwards to Chester, the river forms part of the border between England and Wales.

Top: The road crossing at Langollen was built in 1345 by John Trevor, who became Bishop of St Asaph. It was widened to cross the railway line in the 1860s. *(Tony Hisgett)*

Middle left: The Pontysylite aqueduct is the longest and highest in the country and was built by Thomas Telford and Willam Jessop. Carrying the Llangollen Canal, it was completed in 1805. *(Adrian Pingstone)*

Bottom left: On 24 May 1847, the Chester & Holyhead Railway's bridge over the Dee collapsed, resulting in five deaths. Designed by Robert Stephenson, it was built of girders of cast iron, which is more brittle than wrought iron.

Castle Dinas Bran, Barber's Hill and the Egiwyseg Rocks, form a background unrivalled for picturesque effect, and enclose the vale in an amphitheatre of loveliness. Railways, canals, lime quarries, and the distant iron works, mark the progress of commercial enterprise. Proceeding onwards, with the Chester and Ellesmere canal running for some distance parallel with us, we pass Cefn, with Wynnstay and its pretty park on our right, and the works of the British Iron Company on our left, and arrive at the station of

RUABON

Population, 7,425. A telegraph station. HOTEL – Wynnstay Arms.

The village of Ruabon is most pleasantly situated, and there are mansions, iron and coal works in the neighbourhood. Ruabon Church is well worthy of a visit. It contains several fine monuments particularly one to the memory of Sir Watkin Wm. Wynne, Bart., which is much admired.

VALE OF LLANGOLLEN

Although a very small portion of this line is now open, it leads into the very heart of the picturesque and beautiful. It will traverse the whole length of the Vale of Llangollen and the valley of the Dee up to Corwen, and continue its course from thence to Ruthin and Rhyl, through the Vale of Clwyd, northward, and to Bala, Dolgelly, and Barmouth, westward. From Ruabon the line runs via the stations of
ACREFAIR and TREVOE.

The Vale of Llangollen is said to equal any of the beauties of the Rhine, and it no doubt surpasses them in works of art, the aqueduct and viaduct being splendid ornaments to this lovely work of nature.

LLANGOLLEN

Llangollen lies in the hollow of the Dee, called in Welsh, Glyndurdwy, i.e., valley of the Dyfyrdwy; and being the first glimpse of peculiar mountain scenery which the visitor comes upon, it is indebted to this as much as to its own character for the celebrity it enjoys. The population of the parish is 5,799, including some engaged in the flannel and woollen manufacture. Plasnewydd, or New Hall, where the Maid of Llangollen, Lady E. Butler, and her friend (so graphically delineated by the late Charles Matthews), Miss Ponsonby, lived in happy retirement, remains in the same state as when occupied by them. The two former residents are buried in the old Gothic church, which is dedicated to Saint Collett, whose full name is Collen ap Gwynnciwg ap Cwynnawg ap Cowdra ap Caradoc Freichfas ap Lleyr Merion ap Einion Yrth ap Cunedda Wledig. What an affliction to have to invoke the saint by his full name, or to be christened after him! A Gothic Bridge in four arches is as old as the 14th century. The Vale is best seen in the evening light, but the 'Vale of the Cross at its upper end – which is generally confounded with it – and that of Llandysilio, on the Holyhead road, opposite the former, are both superior to Llangollen.' (Cliffe's *North Wales*). It lies between hills in which limestone and coal, and in other parts excellent slate, are quarried. What the latter article will bear may be seen from the slabs laid down opposite St Mildred's, in the Poultry, London; the grain is so firm, that though millions of feet have passed over that pavement, it is as smooth and sound as ever.

Opposite the bridge the hills rise upwards of 900 feet high, and are surmounted by the remains of an old British fortress, which commanded the pass, called Castle Dinas Bran (dinas means a fort). A winding path leads to it from the Tower farm. Going down the Dee, you come to Plas-y-Pentre, a seat between the river and the canal, below which is the Pont-y-Cysylltan, or aqueduct which carries the Ellesmere canal over the valley.

A little above Llangollen is Valle Crucis, or the Valley of the Cross, which may be ascended to view the striking remains of an abbey, founded in the 13th century, beyond which is the more ancient Cross called Eliseg, which gives name to the pass. The road leads hence over Craig Eglwyseg, and other peaks 1,500 to 1,800 feet high, to the head of the Vale of Clwydd, and to Ruthin and Denbigh Castles.

Down the Dee, below the Cysylltan aqueduct is *Wynnstay*, the hospitable and extensive mansion of Sir W. W. Wynne, Batt., in a beautiful park of 9 miles circuit. Watt's dyke intersects the grounds, in which are an obelisk 101 feet high, a cenotaph to the memory of those soldiers who fell in the Irish rebellion of '98, and a tower to commemorate the victory of Waterloo. Since writing the above, the mansion has been totally destroyed, with its very valuable contents, by fire. Still higher up the Dee are, *Llantysilio Hall*, seat of A. Reid, Esq., near the canal reservoir; and (at the 7th mile stone) *Glyndwr's Mount*, marking the site of Sycharth, or Sychuant, the seat of the famous Owen Glyndwr, or Glendower, whose county this was. A mile or two further is *Corwen Church*, a half Norman building. A cross in the church yard is called Owen Glyndwr's sword; a dagger which belonged to that chief is at Col. Vaughan's seat, *Rhug*. The great Holyhead road here strikes off through the mountains to Capel Curig (26 miles), Snowdon and Bangor; while another follows the Dee to Bala Lake (13 miles), which has its source in the Arran Mowddwy mountains. These range 2,950 feet high at the most, and fall as a continuation of the Berwyn mountains, which appear nearer Llangollen, and at Moel Ferna (Moel means bald), within a few miles of it, are 2,100 feet high, and at Cader Berwyn, about 2,560 feet high. Under this last point (12 miles south-west) is the famous waterfall of Pistyll Rhaiadyr. Here in a dark well-wooded hollow one of the head springs of the Tanat.

WREXHAM

A telegraph station. HOTEL – Wynnstay Arms.

Post horses, flys, etc., at the station and Tariff – 1s 6d per mile, post boy 3d per mile. MARKET DAYS – Thursday and Saturday.

WREXHAM is a populous town in the county of Denbigh. Population 7,562, who return one member. It stands in a fertile plain adjoining Royal Vale of Cheshire. It is well built, the church is a very handsome edifice, built in the 15th century and is equal in point of beauty to many of our cathedrals. It is 178 feet long, 72 feet wide, and has a tower 185 feet in height, which portion is sidered a masterpiece of architectural display; it contains a chaste monument by Roubiliac to Mary Middleton, with some fine monuments of the neighbouring gentry. In addition to this edifice there are several other places of worship. The town being situated in the centre of an extensive mining manufacturing district is considered the metropolis of North Wales. The town-hall is a large edifice at the top of High Street.

In the vicinity is *Gardden Lodge*, the seat of G. Walmsley, Esq., on a hill to the right, built on the site of an old fortress and encampment, in the vicinity of which a battle was fought between the English and the Welsh in 1161–2.

At Holt (6 miles) there are an interesting stone bridge, of ten arches, over the Dee, erected in the 14th century; some remains of an extensive and Roman earthworks. At Bangor Iscoed are the vestiges of a British college, which was founded by King Lucius in 180, and contained 2,400 monks, 1,200 of whom were slain, unarmed, on a battle near Chester, by Ethelfrith.

The train now traverses for a considerable distance what is called 'free' or neutral ground where at one time trade and commerce could only be transacted between the ancient Britons, the Danes, and afterwards the Saxons.

Recrossing Watt's Dyke, we arrive at the junction of the

BRYNABO, MINERA, ETC., BRANCH

This mineral branch diverges to the right, and passes across the coalfield to the lime rocks of Minera. It is 6¼ miles in length. There are several smaller branches made for the accommodation of the works at Frood; Brynmally, Westminster, South Sea, Brymbo, and Vron, to the extent of about 6 miles in addition.

At a place called Wheatsheaf the locomotive portion of the branch terminates, and the lower self-acting inclined plane commences, by which the loaded wagons descend, and draw up the empty ones to Summerhill level. At Summerhill the branch pierces the crest of a hill by a tunnel, and enters the Moss Valley, which is here a narrow ravine, beautifully wooded, having its sides studded with cottages and gardens, which are chiefly small freeholds, the property of the workmen.

From Moss Valley the main branch rises by a steep inclined plane to Peutre, at an inclination of 1 in 4. At the top it pierces through the summit of the Peutre by a tunnel, on emerging from which is Brymbo Valley and iron works. From the tunnel the railway winds its course for about 4 miles to Minera, celebrated for its lead mines and limestone rocks. As the railway winds along the slope of the hills a most magnificent panoramic view is obtained, extending from the Mersey, dotted with white sails, across the Vale Royal, over Cheshire and Shropshire to the Severn, flanked on the left by the Hope Mountains, and on the right by the Berwyn range, to which succeed the Brydden, the Wrekin, Caer Caradoc, and the distant Cheshire hills; and while the eye is charmed with the beauty of the landscape, the mineral treasures and the varied mechanical contrivances by which their value is brought out, commands the attention and admiration of the geologist and scientific visitor.

Snowdonia

Above and left: Two coloured views of the Snowdon Massif, *c.* 1895. Snowdonia, known to the Welsh as Eryri, became the first of the three National Parks in Wales in 1951. Snowdon is the highest mountain in Wales and is 3,560 feet high. The Snowdon Mountain Railway is a narrow gauge rack and pinion railway completed in 1896. The opening day on 6 April was marred by the death of a passenger when No. 1 *Ladas* ran out of control and the train derailed.

Flint

Left: The keep at Flint Castle. This was one of a series of castles built during Edward I's campaign to conquer Wales. The railway station at Flint opened on 1 May 1848 on the Chester & Holyhead Railway. The station building was refurbished in 2007 and is a fine example by the architect Francis Thompson.

PRINCIPALITY OF WALES

We are now approaching the Welsh Mountains; the Clwydian Hills are seen in the distance; the one in the centre called Moel Fammau, or the Mother of Hills, is the loftiest, on the top of which is a jubilee column, erected to commemorate the fiftieth anniversary of the reign of George III. The view front this elevation is most varied and extensive, comprising the Derbyshire Hills, the Wrekin in Shropshire, Snowdon, and Cader Idris in Wales, as well as the Cumberland Hills, and in clear weather even the Isle of Man.

Continuing our route, we pass, on the left, the branch railway to Mold, and shortly after reach Sandycroft, where there is a large foundry. Two miles to the left of this are seen the town and castle of Hawarden. There are several coal mines in the neighbourhood, and in the vicinity of Buckley are earthenware manufactories of considerable repute.

Proceeding onwards, we soon reach QUEEN'S FERRY station (Flintshire). On leaving this station the line passes through deep cuttings and a short tunnel, and immediately afterwards we have a fine view of the estuary of the Dee, which at high tide assumes the appearance of an arm of the sea, covered at times with innumerable vessels.

About a mile to the left is the mansion of Edward Bates, Esq., which commands a particularly fine view of the estuary and the Cheshire shore.

A little further on is *Leadbrook*, so named from the profusion of lead ore obtained in the neighbourhood and the adjacent hills, particularly in the Halkin Mountain, the metallic productions of which have been immense; one spot alone having yielded, in the space of a few years, upwards of a million sterling in value. The porcelain clay at Halkin is also considered very fine.

FLINT

Telegraph station at Chester, 12½ miles. HOTEL – The Oak.
FAIRS – 1st Monday in February, July & Nov. 3rd.

This station is situated in the centre of the town, which is a sea port and market town, with a population of 3,428, who return one member, as well as the county itself. There are extensive collieries, the coals from which are shipped from here to Liverpool, Ireland, and various parts of Wales. The ruins of Flint Castle are seen on the right, at no very great distance from the railway, situated on a rock which juts out towards the sea. It is a memento of other ages, and is peculiarly rich in historical associations, one of the most celebrated events connected with it being the deposition of Richard II. The castle is but a mere shell, there being left only the grey ruined walls, and the two outside concentric walls with the gallery, to attest its former strength and grandeur.

On leaving the station the line proceeds over Flint Marsh, to the left of which is Coles Hill, where a battle was fought, between Owen Gwyndwr and Henry II, in which the latter was defeated.

The next station we come to is ...

BAGILLT

Telegraph station at Chester, 14½ miles.

During the last twenty years this town has become of some importance, in consequence of several very extensive collieries and lead works which have been established here. A large portion of the lead ore produced in the different parts of the kingdom are brought here for smelting. On the hill to the left are seen the ruins of Basingwerk Abbey, built by the Earls of Chester, beautifully situated just above the road, and commanding extensive views of the River Dee, Hilbree Island, etc. Close at hand is Bagillt Hall, the fine old seat of the Griffiths.

HOLYWELL

Telegraph station at Rhyl, 15¼ miles. HOTEL – White Horse.

MARKET DAY – Friday. FAIRS: June 22nd and November 3rd. Races in Autumn.

The important town of Holywell is situated about a mile from the station. Population 5,335, and built on the declivity of a hill, which gradually extends to Greenfield, the surrounding hill forming a kind of amphitheatre. It is one of first towns in North Wales, in a commercial point of view. The far-famed Holy Well of St Winifrede is worthy of a pilgrimage, its architecture is so rich, and well repays a halt at the station to go and visit it. The town owes its origin to this well, its stream having been made available to turn the machinery of extensive mills and manufactories; some of which are closed, but the Holy Well is as strong as ever in all its purity, ever gushing and throwing up eighty-five hogsheads of water per minute, as brilliantly clear as possible. It is visited by numbers of persons, who test its efficacy by the enjoyment of restored health. As a cold bath, perhaps, it is unequalled. Small cabins are built for the convenience of persons wishing to bathe. There are several paper mills in the vicinity.

A short distance further on, concealed in a wood, is the seat of Lord Fielding, the views from which are exceedingly fine, particularly that towards the sea. The next object that attracts attention is Christ Church, situated on a delightful rural eminence above the estuary of the Dee.

MOSTYN QUAY and STATION

Telegraph station at Rhyl, 10 miles.

This place has become of considerable importance from the collieries in the neighbourhood, produce about 70,000 tons annually, and which are considered the most extensive works in all the coal fields of Flintshire, and extend from east to west about 20 miles. About half a mile on the left is *Modes Hall*, at which is the window through which Henry VII escaped from Richard III, and the family pedigree, 42 feet in length, traced from Adam, the mansion of the late Hon. E. M. L. Mostyn, one of the oldest families in North Wales.

Leaving this station the train passes over Gwespyr Marsh, which was enclosed from the sea in 1811, On the right, and nearly in the centre of the estuary of the Dee, is situated Hilbree Island, and in the same direction Hoylake, the extreme point of the peninsula of Wirral, in Cheshire.

The village of *Gwespyr*, celebrated for its quarries of freestone, is situated on the hill to the left. The Custom House of Liverpool is built of the stone from these quarries.

Talacre, the beautiful seat of Sir Pyers Mostyn, Bart., is situated on a gentle eminence. It is a very splendid mansion with two fronts, and commands magnificent views of the sea. The village on the hill is Gronant; above which is the Observatory. On the right, close to the shore, is the life boat house.

PRESTATYN

Telegraph station at Rhyl, 3¾ miles.

Here the country is flat, but extremely fertile in corn, especially wheat, and continues so as far as Rhuddlan, and thence along the coast to Abergele.

Proceeding onward we pass the village of Melidan, with its rural Church, on the left; close to which, under a rock, are situated the Talargoch Lead Mines celebrated as having produced more lead ore than any other mine in the country during the last century, the quantity raised averaging 3,000 tons annually. The ruins of Dyserth Castle, built in Henry II's time, are in the vicinity; and a mile beyond which is Bodryddon, the ancient seat of the Conways, situated in a fine forest.

RHYL

A telegraph station. HOTELS – The Mostyn Arms; the Royal; Belvoir; George; Queen's. MARKET DAY – Tuesday. Supplied profusely every day in the season.

RHYL is a fashionable watering place for the North 'Wailians' and Liverpool people; it is reputed one of the best bathing places in Wales. The beauty of the scenery, salubrity of the air, and firmness of the sand, render it a place of considerable attraction to visitors from all parts of the kingdom. It is situated at the entrance of the celebrated vale of Clwyd, which extends 20 miles in length, and about 10 miles in breadth, flanked on both sides with elevated hills. Snowdon can be seen.

In addition to the hotels and inns there are hundreds of elegant and respectable lodging houses, capable of affording excellent accommodation for visitors, at very moderate charges. There are bathing establishments and machines in abundance.

On the left of Rhyl are the celebrated range of British Posts, on the Clwydian Hills; established as a bulwark against an invading enemy.

VALE OF CLWYD

Ehyl to Ruthin

The district through which this line runs is remarkable for its picturesque beauty, and forms the threshold to some of the richest scenery in North Wales. Passing quickly the little station of FORYD, the arrival of the train is soon announced at the ancient town of

RHUDDLAN

Population, 1,406. FAIRS – First Tuesday in February and May, and last Tuesday in July and October, and the Tuesday before the 25th December.

The town is situated on the eastern bank of the river Clwyd. Below it is Rhuddlan Castle, the ruins of which have a noble and imposing appearance from every point of view. The historical reminiscences connected with this fortress are of great interest, but too voluminous and ancient for our general readers. It was built by Llewellyn in 1015, and dismantled in 1646. In the church are tombs of Dean Shipley and the Conways. A mile from the castle is *Pengwern*, the seat of Lord Mostyn, most delightfully situated in the vale of Clwyd.

ST ASAPH

Population, 2,063.

The city of St Asaph is situated on a delightful eminence between the streams, near the confluence of the rivers Elwy and Clwyd. The principal attraction of this city is the Cathedral, which was first built of wood in 596, by St Asaph, and rebuilt in 1770. The plan of the church is like most others cruciform, with a square embattled tower rising from the intersection of the nave and transepts. The visitor on entering the sacred edifice will be struck with the solemnity which pervades the building; the chastened light, entering from the richly painted windows, evidently copied from those of Tintern Abbey, throws a softened tint over the Gothic stalls

Above: Regarded as the first major rail disaster in the country, on 20 August 1868 an LNWR Irish Mail train hit runaway wagons from a goods train between Abergele and Llanddulas, resulting in thirty-three deaths.

and chequered pavement of the choir, which to the eye capable of appreciating the beauty of the scene is highly pleasing and interesting. It contains tombs of Bishops ap Owen in 1512, and Barrow, the uncle of the celebrated Boac Barrow. The most eminent prelates of this see were Parry, Morgan (who translated the Bible into Welsh), Tanner, Beveridge, and Horsley.

The Episcopal Palace is an ancient one, rebuilt by the late bishop. The neighbourhood of St Asaph is studded with a variety of gentlemen's seats, among which are *Pengwern*, Lord Mostyn; *Kinmel*, Lord Dinorben; and *Bodelwyddan*, Sir J. Williams, Bart.

Trefnant Station, Denbighshire.

DENBIGH

Population 5,946. HOTELS – Bull; Crown.

The situation of this town from a distance is very imposing, lying as it does on the side of a rocky eminence, the top of which is crowned with the ruins of a castle founded in the reign of Edward I. It was blown up with gunpowder after the restoration of Charles II. The prospect from its ruins is of a magnificent character.

LLANRHAIDR and RHEWL Stations.

Ruthin, a market town, standing on the slope of a hill. It has the remains of a castle, built in the 13th century.

Chester & Holyhead Main line continued, Rhyl to Conway

Upon leaving, the Rhyl station the line proceeds on an embankment and drawbridge over the river Foryd. The extensive tract of land on the left is the celebrated spot where the battle of Rhuddlan Marsh took place in 785; this marsh was secured from the encroachments of the sea in 1799, enclosing about 27,000 acres of sandy loam land.

The village on the hill is called St George, or Llan St Sior.

ABERGELE

POPULATION, 3,309. Telegraph station at Rhyl, 43 miles.

HOTELS – The Bee, Mrs Clarke, is the best house; has very good accommodation for visitors, and can be well recommended. There are pleasure grounds connected with the house, which is within easy walking distance from the shore. MARKET DAY – Saturday. FAIRS – Feb. 12th, April 2nd, day before Holy Thursday, June 18th, October 9th. and Dec. 6th.

This station is close to the seaside, and at a little distance from the town. Its situation is very beautiful, the Clwydian range of hills forming a most picturesque and varied back ground to it; and *Gwrych Castle*, the elegant seat of Lloyd Bamford Hesketh, Esq., adding a peculiar charm to the whole. It consists of only one wide street, but the salubrity of the air, and its sea shore, render it a favourite watering place for bathing. The scenery in the neighbourhood is magnificent, and is adorned with gentlemen's seats and thickly-wooded parks. In the vicinity are British and Roman camps, Cefn Oge cave, where Richard II lay concealed until betrayed to Bolingbroke by Percy, and the Lysfaen telegraph 709 feet high, which communicates with Liverpool.

From Abergele the railway keeps close to the seaside for some distance, and then winds round to Conway. On proceeding onward from the Abergele station, we observe some huge rocks on the right, some miles before us, which are called the Great Orme's Head, a high promontory, projecting from the main land into the sea. We next pass the village of Llandulas, sitrated in a glen surrounded with lime-stone rocks. Nearly 100,000 tons of stone are extracted from the quarries here, and shipped annually to all parts of the country.

On emerging from the Penmaen Rhos tunnel, we see the village of COLWYN on the left; and farther on up the valley, that of Llanelian, celebrated for its Cursing Well or Ffynnon Eilian. Further on towards the shore, is the village of Llandrilio, formerly the residence of a British King.

Proceeding onwards on the left is seen the newly erected mansion of Sir Thomas Erskine, Bart. The line then passes through the small vale Mochtre, and winds round in the direction of Conway to LLANDUDNO JUNCTION, the point of deviation of the ST GEORGE'S HARBOUR.

Above: Postcard showing the Llandudno pier. Note the paddle steamer.

Above: Llandudno Junction signal box. *(RuthAS)*

Conway to Llandudno

The distant landscapes and marine views presented to the eye of the tourist as he passes along this little line, commanding as it does the full scope of the beautiful Bay of Beaumaris, are of a most varied and interesting character. In ten minutes after passing the junction the arrival of the train is announced at

LLANDUDNO

Telegraph station at Conway, 3½ miles.

This delightful place has now become one of great importance as a summer resort. It is situated 31 miles from Conway, on a promontory between the Bays of Conway and Llandudno. The water is very clear, and affords excellent bathing, and being protected on the north by the Great Orme's Head, the air is peculiarly salubrious. The old Church (dedicated to St Tudno) stands on the mountain side. A new church was erected about 1839; but this is found much too small for the increasing requirements of the bathing season. There is also a fine market, well supplied with fish, vegetables, and in fact everything calculated to render the comforts of a termporary sojourn complete.

The scenery around is most picturesque, particularly so from the promenade which skirts the outer margin of the top of the mountain, at a height of 676 feet. The views from this point arc of the most fascinating character. The town itself is in the very heart of the most attractive parts of North Wales. It can boast of some good water excursions, embracing some curious and picturesque eaves both on the Great and Little Orme's Head.

Chester & Holyhead Railway

The C&HR was devised to enable the Irish Mail trains to travel from London, via the West Coast Main Line, across north Wales to connect with the steam packets at Holyhead.

Left: The station interior at Chester.

HOLYHEAD STATION.
PASSENGERS EMBARKING FOR DUBLIN (NORTH WALL)

Through trains from Chester to Bangor started in May 1848, and through trains to Holyhead followed two years later with the completion of the Britannia Bridge. *Above:* The clock tower on Holyhead Docks. *(RuthAS)* *Left:* Two postcard views of the dockside station at Holyhead.

HOLYHEAD STATION–EASY TRANSFER, TRAIN & STEAMER.

Retracing our steps to Llandudno Junction, we take another turn along the ...
CONWAY & LLANRWST.

Which here diverges to the left. The valley through which this line passes is described by Burke as 'the most charming spot in North Wales'. It skirts the eastern bank of the Conway, following its various windings. At a distance of two miles beyond the junction we come to the station of LLANSAINT-FRAIDD, the village of which consists of a number of cottages scattered over the side of the hill, to the left of the line. From this point the line passes frequently beneath well-timbered cliffs, on the one hand, and the silent stream on the other, until we arrive at the next station.

TAL-Y-CEFN. Here is a ferry across the river into Carnarvonshire, and in the immediate vicinity two waterfalls, the Porthlwyd and Dolgarrog, the former of which should be seen.

LLANRWST

HOTEL – The Gwydir Arms.

LLANRWST, once noted for its Welsh harpmakers, lies on the east bank of the River Conway, about 12 miles from Conway, and is situated in one of the prettiest spots of North Wales. It ought not to be overlooked.

In the vicinity is Trefriw, in a hollow of the Carnarvonshire hills, where there are some salubrious mineral waters. One of the Inland Company's steamers makes the trip to Conway every week day during the summer months. This trip affords some really fine and much-commended views of the valley of the Conway, every bend of the river disclosing some hitherto undiscovered loveliness.

Holyhead Main Line continued

Returning once more to Llandudno Junction we again take our seats, and pursuing our course along the main line, suddenly approach the river, where a most magnificent landscape presents itself. The fine old town of Conway, with its ancient castles, walls, and towers, appears in front, and the vast range of the Carnarvonshire mountains forming a back ground, has a beautiful effect. The line runs on an embankment several hundred yards parallel with the turnpike road, and then crosses the broad expanse of the river, through the tubular bridge, that wonder of modern engineering skill, and after a few seconds of darkness we emerge into daylight, beneath the lofty shattered walls of Conway Castle. Sweeping round the base of the castle on a circle, the railway glides on and enters the town of Conway, under a pointed arch constructed in the old walls of the town. This arch gives great picturesqueness of effect to the station, which adjoins it; and the castellated character of the wall is preserved by the battlements upon it. The station is an extremely handsome and well-designed building, in the Elizabethan style, with gabled wings, rising in steps, and projecting from the main portion.

Durable and Delightful

"The **Conway** Serge"

INDIGO BLUE HERRINGBONE
PURE WOOL GUARANTEED COLOUR

Conwy's Bridges

Crossing over the River Conwy there are three bridges: the modern road bridge, Telford's suspension bridge (the old road bridge) of 1826, shown above, and Stephenson's single span tubular rail bridge of wrought-iron, which was built to a design by William Fairbairn and completed in 1849. *Below:* All three are shown in this photograph taken from the castle. *(Bencherlite)*

Population, 2,523. A telegraph station. HOTEL – Castle.

MARKET DAY – Friday. FAIRS – March 26th, April 30th, June 30th, August 10th, September 10th, and October 20th.

The ancient town of Conway is within the walls that were erected at the same time as the castle, and which are ornamented with circular towers. Although not a manufacturing town, it has always been a place of some importance. The vale through which the River Conway flows, is remarkable for its beauty and fertility. Its luxuriant pastures, corn fields, and groves, are finely contrasted with the bleak appearance of Snowdon mountain, which towers in frowning majesty above it.

Conway Castle, which belongs to the Marquis of Hertford, stands on a rock which rises considerably above the river. It was built in 1284, by King Edward I, to check the frequent revolts of the Welsh. The walls are of enormous thickness, and defended by eight massive round towers. The great hall of the castle measures 130 feet in length. The King's Chamber, as it is called, occupying one of the circular towers contiguous to the river, has a very pretty Gothic window, which seems to be the only part of the castle where any degree of ornament has been attempted. Richard II, when he fled from Ireland, in 1339, took refuge in this castle, where he agreed with the Earl of Northumberland and the Archbishop of Canterbury, to resign the crown to the Duke of Lancaster. From this circumstance arose the civil wars which desolated the country for so long a period. In St Mary's church is a carved black font, screen, stained glass window, and tomb of Nicholas Hookes, whose father had forty-one children, and his wife brought him twenty-seven.

The most favourable view of the castle and bridge is obtained a few hundred yards higher up the river, on the same side. Here it is seen boldly projecting in the foreground, with the beautiful new suspension bridge attached. Part of the town appears on the left, while the mouth of the river, open to the sea, forms the distance, which, with the vessels of various descriptions gliding on the surface, forms one of the most charming pictures that the imagination can conceive. There are several very attractive places in the neighbourhood of Conway, and a traveller may spend several days very pleasantly here in making excursions to the various places in the vicinity, viz., to the ruins of Gannock Castle, the walks of Gloddaeth, etc., etc.

The iron Tubular Bridge, erected in 1848 by Stephenson, over the Conway, is one of the most unique examples of engineering skill ever imagined or carried into execution. Though inferior in length and weight to the Britannia Bridge, yet being built on precisely the same principles, and raised to its destined site by the same power, it may, from the circumstance of its having been the first erected, be deemed an original idea, beautifully carried out to its fullest extent in its mighty contemporary. The tubular viaduct over the Conway consists of two tubes, placed in juxta-position, one for the up, and the other for the down trains, each of them measuring 400 feet in length, and weighing 1,300 tons. Its section is nearly rectangular, with a slight arch at the top to prevent the accumulation of rain. Its walls are formed of a series of iron plates, composed entirely of hard wrought iron, varying from half-an-inch to an inch in thickness; the greater strength being in the middle.

Upon leaving Conway station, the line proceeds through a tunnel under one of the towers, and thence through some deep cuttings to Conway Marsh. We then cross the Holyhead road, and pass old Conway race course on the right. Looking across the estuary the traveller will have a fine view of the ruins of Gannock Castle and Great Orme's Head. The railway then skirts the sea shore again, until it enters Penmaen Bach Tunnel, on emerging from which we perceive Penmaen Mawr, the terminating point of the Carnarvonshire range of mountains. On the summit of this hill are the ruins of an extensive fortress. It is surrounded by strong treble walls, within each of which are the foundation sites of more than 100 round towers, with ample room for 20,000 men.

PENMAEN MAWR station; the mountain is 1,540 feet high, and Penmaen Bach hill, 837 feet.

Proceeding onwards we pass in succession Penmaen Mawr tunnel, and Meini Merlon, one of the most remarkable mountains in all Snowdon. On the right is Puffin Island, inhabited by vast numbers of birds called puffins. The railway continues for some time further along the sea shore.

The village of ADEE, celebrated as being the last place where Llewellyn contended against Edward I, is a most delightful spot; having on the right the view of the Irish Channel, in front, Beaumaris and its wooded environs, and to the left the turrets of Penrhyn Castle. From this village, a deep and romantic glen,

The entrance to the medieval castle at Conwy.
Built by Edward I between 1283 and 1289, it has been classed by UNESCO as a World Heritage Site. (LoC)

nearly 3 miles in length, forms the avenue to Rhaiadr Mawr, a celebrated cataract. The prospects in the neighbourhood afford views of most picturesque beauty, comprising the Snowdon mountains on the one hand, the Menai straits and the coast of Anglesey on the other, all together forming a rich panoramic view of splendid scenery.

The railway is then carried over the Ogwen river and valley by two extensive viaducts, commanding beautiful views of the surrounding scenery. The train shortly enters the Bangor tunnel, through Bangor mountain, and, on emerging from it, arrives at ...

BANGOR

A telegraph station. HOTELS – The George, Bangor Ferry, Miss Roberts, is a first-class house, delightfully situated between Bangor and Menai Bridge, and is deservedly celebrated for its excellent arrangements. The British, W. Dew, a favourite establishment, highly spoken of for its arrangements and general management. It has one of the finest coffee-rooms in North Wales. The Penrhyn Arms, Charles Bicknell, is a first-class establishment for families and gentlemen, and, from the high standing it has maintained for a series of years, may with confidence be recommended. MARKET DAY – Friday.
FAIRS – April 5th, June 25th, September 16th, and October 28th.

A cathedral town and bathing place in Carnarvonshire, North Wales, near Snowdon, and only 2¼ miles from the Britannia Bridge. You enter it by a tunnel 3,000 feet long. It is an excellent resting place, not only for the fine mountain scenery of this quarter, but for the Britannia and Menai Bridges, the Penrhyn State Quarries, Beaumaris Castle, and other excursions, by road, railway, and boat. More than 50,000 persons come here in the season, so that lodgings at such times are high and difficult to be had. About forty years ago there were only ninety houses, now there are 1,336, to a population of 6,738.

The 'city' is chiefly a long street, winding about under the rocks towards Garth Point, where there is the public promenade, besides a ferry over the Lavan Sands to Beaumaris, on the Anglesey side. The peaks round Snowdon, and the rocky headlands of Penmaen Mawr and Orme's Head are in view. Among the buildings are the Assembly Rooms, Shone's Library, County Dispensary, Glynne's Grammar School, and a small plain cathedral, 23 feet long, with a low tower, not older than the 15th century – the former one having been burnt by Owen Gwyndwr or Glendower. It was originally founded by St Detliol, as early as 550, whence Bangor claims to be the oldest diocese in Wales. The income is £4,000 per annum. This argument was used when there was a talk of suppressing it some years back. There are tombs of two Welsh princes, Gryfydd (or Griffith) ap Cynan and Owen Gwyndwr; and, a new painted window placed here by Dean Cotton, through whose exertions the church has been restored. It is the parish church to the town, the service being in Welsh. In the library is the missal and anthem book of Bishop Anian, who held the see in Edward I's time. Another bishop was Hoadley, appointed by George I; he preached a sermon here from the text, 'My kingdom is

Above: A coloured lithograph of a Chester & Holyhead Railway train pulling into Bangor, *c.* 1850.

not of this world', so displeasing to the high church party, that it gave rise to a long dispute – the celebrated Bangorian Controversy.

A British camp and part of a castle may be seen on two points, near Friar's School. Further south is *Vaenol*, the seat of the late Assheton Smith, a mighty hunter in Hampshire, and owner of the Dinorwie Slate Quarries, under Snowdon. About 30,000 tons are annually sent down to Port Dinorwie by railway, and 1,000 hands employed. Opposite, on the Anglesey side, is Plas Newydd, the seat of the Marquis of Anglesey, for many months the residence of the Duchess of Kent and Princess Victoria. It has the Anglesey pillar, fixed on Waterloo day in 1816, with a cairn, and an immense Druid cromlech. Anglesey was the last and most famous seat of Druid worship.

One mile east of Bangor, is *Penrhyn Castle*, the seat of Colonel Pennant, proprietor of the famous Penrhyn Slate Quarries, worth £70,000 a year: it is an extensive Norman pile, built by Wyatt, of Anglesey marble; and open on Fridays to the public. As may be supposed, many curious articles in slate are to be seen. The park fence, seven miles round, is all of that fabric.

The Penrhyn Slate Quarries are about 5 miles up the river Ogwen, under Snowdon, following the tramway, and well deserve a visit. You pass Llandegai Gothic Church, with the tomb of Lord Penrhyn, a great benefactor of this neighbourhood, who made the slate works what they are. He spent £170,000 on the shipping port alone. An inclined plane leads up to the edge of the vast mountain, on the sides of which above 2,000 hands are employed in hacking and splitting. The slates are trimmed and piled in thousands according to their size, under the names of duchesses. countesses, ladies, etc.; and are used for roofing, gravestones, schools, and other purposes. They have a fine smooth grain; many of the chapels and houses about here are wholly built of that slate which is shipped at Port Penrhyn (close by) to all parts of the world, to the extent of 70,000 tons yearly. The gross receipts may be calculated at £150,000 a year.

From the slate works the road ascends the wild pass of Nant Francon or Beaver valley, between the Glyder Fawr and Carnedd Dafydd, the latter a peak of the Snowdon range, 3,420 feet high. Carnedd Llewelyn to the north of it is 3,469 feet. The road crosses the Ogwen at the Benglog Falls, which are at the outlet of Llyn or Lake Ogwen, where a stream joins them from Llyn Idwal situate in a most gloomy hollow up the sides of Glyder Fawr, a peak to the south 3,300 feet high (you may wind over it past a gap called the Twll Du or Devil's Kitchen and Llyn-y-Cwm to Llanberis). It is a difficult path, but offers fine prospects. From Ogwen lake the road descends to

Capel Curig. A pretty spot on the Llagay, near the two Mymbyr Lakes, 14 miles from Bangor. The village, not in itself very important, beyond the facilities it affords to the tourist as a centre from whence some of the most charming excursions may be made, being situated in the very heart of the most splendid lake and mountain scenery that North Wales can boast of. The views of Snowdon are here truly magnificent. Hence down the pretty Llagwy past Rhayadr-y-Wennol fall to Bettws-y-Coed in a green sheltered nook of the Conway 6 miles further, is a resort well known to anglers and artists.

From the Slate Works to the tops of Carnedd Dafydd and Carnedd Llewelyn is a fatiguing walk of 4 to 6 or 7 miles; but there is a grand prospect from both. To Delwyddellan Castle, under Moel Siabod, 2,870 feet, and thence on to the vale of Ffestiniog requires a walk of 18 miles from Capel Curig.

The carriage road winds round the east base of Snowdon, passing Trafaen (so called from the three stones l5 feet high on the top) and the Glyder Bach or Little Glyder, 3,000 feet high, and joined to Glyder Fawr or Great Glyder, by the Waenoer, a desolate plain half a mile wide, covered with weather beaten stones. Moel Siabod or Shabod is on the southeast side. At Nant-y-Gwryd Inn, a road branches off to Beddgelert, 12 miles from Capel Curig, passing Llyn Gwynant, etc. Following the main road through Snowdon you come to the famous Llanberis Pass, a narrow and rugged defile, about three miles long, between the perpendicular cliffs of Glyder Fawr on the north and Snowdon on the south. It is united by the Seiont, which runs down to Carnarvon, and resembles the wild pass of Glencoe in Argyleshire, or the Gap of Dunloe near Killarney. Blocks of rock lie about on all sides. One immense heap called the Cromlech was turned into a sort of house by a herdwoman. It is near the Gorphwysfa or resting place at the top of the ascent front Capel Curig. Two miles further, in a quiet glen, is ...

LLANBERIS
HOTELS – The Victoria; the Dolhadarn.

Narrow Gauge Action
Top left: On the Ffestiniog Railway, trains passing at Tan-y-Bwlch station, *c.* 1900. *(LoC)* The line was built to transport slate from the quarries to the ships at Porthmadog. Today the main cargo is tourists.
Left: Preserved steam at Tan-y-Bwlch. This is the locomotive *Merddin Emrys. (Peter Trimming)*

Below: The Llanberris terminal of the Snowdon Mountain Railway. *(Denis Egan)*

Here is a pretty later English church, enclosing the original timber structure dedicated of St Peris. It stands near Llyn Peris, in the very heart of the mountains, which appear here in all their native majesty. From Llanberis to the top of Snowdon is 31 miles. Two miles further, between Lake Peris and Lake Badarn, there is an old ruined castle with which the Britons used to guard the pass, behind which the Ceunant Mawr Fall rolls down from Moel Aeliau. On the opposite side under the Glyder Fawr are the Dinorwic Slate Quarries, taking name from the Roman fort of Dinas Dinorwig lower down.

From Dolbadarn to the top of Snowdon is 5 to 6 miles, or a two hours' walk. Ponies and guides may be hired at Llanberis, but a stout pair of legs is the best help for those who choose to dispense with such assistants. Start early in the morning when the air is cool. For those who wish to see the sun rise a few huts, accommodated with beds, are built on the top; but it is frequently obscured by clouds. Snowdon is composed of four great ridges of slate and porphyry, viz: Moel Aeliau on the west, 1,371 feet, Clawdd-Coch or the Red Dyke on the south, 2,473 feet, Y-Lliwed on the east, and Crib-y-Dystul or the Dripping Point on the north, 3,420 feet. These are separated by vast precipitous cwms (sounded coombes) or hollows, 1,000 feet deep in some parts; and they unite in one peak marked by an ordnance signal pole, called Moel-y-Wyddfa, the Conspicuous Head, 3,570 feet above the sea; the highest point in Wales or England. This is Snowdon proper. Snowdon is a fanciful English name for the whole ridge of the Carnarvonshire mountains. The Welsh call it Eryri or Eagle Top. It is 800 or 1,000 feet below the line of perpetual snow, which in reality lies here only from November to April. The path from Dolbadarn is along the Crib-y-Dystul ridge, past Cwm Brwynog, and Clogwyn-Du-r-Arddu rock, over a lake and near the cliffs where the lamented Rev. Mr Starr fell over In 1856. Then comes a steep part ealled Llechwedd-y-Ry, overlooking the Llanberis pass, and 1½ miles from the top. If the weather is clear you may see the Wicklow mountains, the Isle of Man, the Yorkshire hills, etc., with above twenty lakes in North Wales, all spread out like a map.

Other starting points for Snowdon are from Beddgelert, over Clawdd-Coch, 6 miles; Llyn Cwellyn on the Carnarvon Road, 4 miles; and from Capel Curig, by Cwm Dyli and Llyn Llydiaw, about 14 miles. The last, though the longest and most fatiguing, is said to be the finest route. Rare mountain plants are found on Snowdon.

BEAUMARIS

Population, 2,599. HOTEL – Bulkeley Arms.

Beaumaris, the capital of Anglesey, is beautifully situated at the entrance to the Menai Straits, about 4 miles from Bangor. It has remains of a castle, built in the thirteenth century by Edward I. The chapel and the great hall, 70 feet long, in which Queen Victoria (then princess) with the Duchess of Kent, her mother, attended an Eisteddfod or Bardic meeting in 1832, are still in a state

Carmarthen

Above: Photograph *c.* 1900 of cockle pickers on Carmarthen Ferryside.
Right: Brigstock Terrace, *c.* 1907.
Below: Sunset at Carmarthen Castle. The original castle on this site dates back to around 1094. Destroyed by Llywelyn the Great, it was rebuilt in the thirteenth century.

of preservation. Baron Hall is the fine seat of Sir E. B. W. Bulkeley. Bart.; in the grounds is the curious stone coffin of King John's daughter, Joan, named Llewellyn ap Jorworth, who founded a priory, of which there are remains at Llanvaes. Further on are Penmon Priory and the Mona (Mon is the Welsh name for Anglesey) Marble Quarries. Then Puffin Island Light, near which the *Rothesay Castle* steamer was wrecked in 1831, and 100 lives lost. Further on to the west there is a fine view from a large camp called Bwrdd Arthur or Arthur's Round Table.

CARNARVON BRANCH

Bangor to Carnarvon and Nantile.

The stations on this branch are TREBORTH, Pout Dnionwic (here are the slate quarries belonging to T. A. Smith, Esq., where 1,000 men are constantly employed), and GRIFFITH'S CROSSING.

CARNARVON

Population, 8,512. A telegraph station.

HOTELS – Royal Sportsman; Uxbridge Arms. Market Days – Satarday.

It occupies the site of a Roman town called Segontium, of which there are various relics in the museum. The well-preserved castle, built between 1284 and 1320, is the most interesting object; it covers 21 acres. There are remains of the gateway, the Queen's gates and the Eagle tower in which it is stated Edward II, the first Prince of Wales, was born. It should be mounted for the view. The outer walls are 10 feet thick and guarded by thirteen towers variously shaped. One of them is the town prison.

In the vicinity is Llanberis (8 miles), the most convenient starting point for Snowdon. Hence the tourist may if he wish extend his railway journey via the stations of Bont Nuwydd, Pwllheli Road, Groes Lon, and Pen-y-Groes, the station for Portmadoc, to Nantlle.

Bangor to Holyhead

Upon quitting Bangor station we almost immediately enter the Egyptian arch of Belmont Tunnel, under the Carnarvon mountains, on emerging from which we have a beautiful view of the Menai Straits, with its accompaniments, Telford's Suspension Bridge and the Britannia Tubular Bridge. In viewing the massive towers and lengthened tubes of the latter, its heavy and colossal proportions stand out in striking contrast with the slender and gossamer-like components of its older rival, the Menai Bridge, which is used for ordinary vehicles and foot passengers, both structures being situated within a mile of each other.

The view across the Menai Straits, looking back towards the mainland, with Thomas Telford's suspension bridge on the left, and the Stephenson tubular iron rail bridge on the right. Telford's bridge was completed in 1826 as part of the road from London to Holyhead, now the A5.

Telford Road, Menai Bridge

MENAI BRIDGE

Two miles from Bangor, across the narrow channel which cuts off Anglesey, is best seen from the water below, above which it rises 100 feet, at high tide. It was built by Telford, between 1819 and 1826, to complete the coach route to Holyhead. From pier to pier (each 153 feet high) the main part of the bridge is 550 feet long, and 20 broad, including a carriage road of 12 feet. The first mail coach drove over this in a wintry storm. It is suspended from 16 chains, each having a total length of 1,715 feet, and fastened into 60 feet of solid rock on each side. The total weight of iron is 650 tons; it would bear about 1,300 tons. It is still the longest suspension bridge in this country, but is exceeded by those at Freibourg, in Switzerland (870 feet between the piers, and 167 high), across the Dordogne, near Bordeaux, and over the Danube, at Pesth.

THE BRITANNIA TUBULAR BRIDGE

This magnificent structure was made to carry the Chester and Holyhead Railway across the Menai Straits. Like the beautiful bridge at Conway, it is on the tubular principle, but on a much grander scale, and is one of the most ingenious, daring, and stupendous monuments of engineering skill which modern times have seen attempted. As this gigantic and amazing structure now spans the Menai, connecting the two opposite shores of Carnarvon and the Isle of Anglesey, we may justly express our admiration of it by calling it Mr Stephenson's chef d'oeuvre, but this would scarcely do justice to the remarkable bridge or its great architect, we therefore think it proper to add the following details:

The idea of carrying a railway through a vast tube, originated with Mr Robert Stephenson. It having been found extremely difficult to construct an arch of the immense span required; and as chain bridges were not sufficiently firm for the purpose of railway traffic, Mr Stephenson suggested the application of iron tubes to pass from pier to pier. These tubes may be described as the double barrel of a gun on an immense scale, through which the trains pass and repass, at unslackened speed, as if it were a tunnel through solid rock on land, instead of being elevated a 104 feet above the sea. The suggestion of Mr Stephenson was adopted, and the Britannia Bridge now forms an imperishable monument to his fame. The construction of the bridge, however, attracted crowds of engineers and others to watch the progress of the stupendous work, and to behold the means by which Mr Stephenson triumphed over all the difficulties he had to encounter in a task of such magnitude.

They saw, day by day, with the liveliest satisfaction, the patient putting together of the tubes, the marvellous facility with which they were floated, and the wonderful machinery by which they were elevated to the destined altitude, until the whole was completed and the first trains run through it without its deflecting more than an inch, and there it still stands, scarcely bending to the heaviest trains, stretching itself as it basks in the warmth of the noonday sun, gathering

The Britannia Bridge

Robert Stephenson's innovative design for the Britannia railway bridge incorporated two rectangular wrought iron tubes through which the trains would pass.

Top left: At the 'Conference of Engineers', Stephenson sought the advice of the prominent engineers of the time before the bridge was built. He is shown seated at the table, with Brunel to the far right. *Left:* With one span in place the other is floated into position on pontoons. *Below:* Carved lions guard the entrances to the bridge. The tubes were damaged by fire in 1970 and replaced with conventional steel arches. An upper deck now carries the A55 road.

itself back under the chill of night, bending towards every gleam of sunshine, or shrinking from every passing cloud.

The Britannia Bridge takes its name from a rock which rises about the middle of the stream, and which is bare at low water. Without this advantage the erection of the pier would have been impossible, in consequence of the strength of the current and the local difficulties. The Britannia pier is built on this rock, and even with this advantage from nature the span from each of the principal piers is 463 feet; the entire length of the bridge, 1,560 feet; and the headway at high water 100 feet, which leaves sufficient room for ships to pass under. We close our description with a brief summary of the leading statistics. It is a wrought-iron tube, made of plates riveted together; 104 feet above the water, 1,513 feet long, 14 feet wide (enough for two lines of railway), 26 feet high in the middle, and 19 feet at the sides, with a total weight of 11,400 tons. The total quantity of stone contained in the bridge is 1,400,000 cubic feet; the timber used in the various scaffoldings for the masonry platforms, for the erection of the tubes, etc., was 450,000 cubic feet. The centre pier is 230 feet high; through this it passes by an opening 45 feet long, which, with 460 feet on each side, makes the main part of the bridge 965 feet long. There are two other piers of less height. At each end are carved lions, 25 feet long. Summer heat lengthens the whole fabric about a foot. It was begun in 1846, and the first train went through on the 5th of March, 1850. The great tubes being first riveted together, were floated out on pontoons, and then raised by hydraulic presses into their place. These presses were shown at the Great Exhibition of 1851. A pillar, near Llanfair Church, is a memorial of the only accident which occurred in the prosecution of this remarkable work. From Bangor it is approached by the Belmont tunnel, 2,172 feet long.

Resuming our route from the Britannia Bridge the train enters thence into the Island of Anglesey, passing over an embankment, at the end of which is the Marquis of Anglesey's column, erected to commemorate the eminent military services of the late venerable Marquis of Anglesey. This island is 24 miles long and 17 broad, containing four market towns and seventy-four parishes; square miles, 402: population, 49,000, who jointly return one member. The sea is fertile; the chief products are grain and cattle.

The railway, after passing the station of Llanfair, now runs parallel for some miles with the Holyhead road, passing Plas Pen Myndd, the ancient seat of the ancestors of the Royal House of Tudor.

Further on the line eradually curves in a south-western direction, near which is Tre'r Dryu, or the habitation of the Arch Druid, abounding in rude memorials of the religious rites practised by our forefathers.

The line from Gaerwen crosses the River Cefni, on a noble viaduct of nineteen arches, and shortly after enters the Trefdraeth Tunnel, cut through some very hard rock, on emerging from which a fine view of Carnarvon Bay presents itself across which are seen the Carnarvonshire hills, called the Rivals.

The line now traverses the parish of Llangadwaladr, and arrives at ...

BODORGAN

Telegraph station at Bangor, 13 miles.

On leaving this station the ancient town of Aberffraw may be seen on our left. In the neighbourhood of the town there is a splendid lake, 2 miles in circumference, called Llyn Coron, much frequented by anglers during the summer. Proceeding onwards through ordinary cuttings, over embankments and bridges in succession, we again come in sight of the Holyhead Road, and pass over the river Alaw, on the banks of which, in 1813, was found buried the sepulchral urn containing the remains of Broniventhe, the daughter of Llyr (King Lear), and aunt to the great Caractacus.

The line from Ty Croes runs parallel with the Stanley embankment, which crosses the sands and an arm of the sea. On the right is the mansion of the Hon. W. Owen Stanley, M.P., in Penrhos Park, and a quarter of a mile east of which is Penrhyn, a cliff projecting into the sea.

Beyond VALLEY station, to the right again, are some ancient forts and an obelisk monument, the latter erected to the memory of the late Captain Skinner, formerly master of one of the packets on this station, who lost his life in 1838. We shortly after arrive at

HOLYHEAD (Holyhead Island)

A telegraph station. Population, 6,193. HOTELS – The Royal; the Castle.
MARKET DAY – Saturday.

HOLYHEAD, so called from a monastery founded by St Gybi (sounded Kubby) in the sixth century, is the chief packet station for Ireland, and stands on Holy Island on a

Above: Anglesey's South Stack lighthouse, overlooking the Irish Sea. *(Abbasi_1111)*

94

bay between it and the west side of Anglesey, in North Wales, 64 miles from Dublin. The rail crosses the narrow strait or traeth dividing the island and main land, on an embankment, close to that which supports Telford's coach road, constructed in 1815, and reaches Bangor by way of Shrewsbury, Corwen, and Bettws-y-Coed. Holy Island is about 7 miles long, with a rugged coast, and mines of mons, or variegated marble, sometimes called verd-antique. Rhoscolyn Church, in the south, has a good view of its barren hills. The town, which contains 5,622 inhabitants, has little to show beyond its old church, in the midst of a Roman camp, and a triumphal arch, near the pier, commemorating the passing of George IV, on his visit to Ireland in 1821. Its port, however, deserves particular attention. The present tidal harbour lies within two piers, made by Rennie, the longest of which, opposite Salt Island, is 1,080 feet; from whence the packets start, and here 150 vessels may find shelter; but as it is small, and dries at low water, it is not of sufficient capacity. But the Great Harbour of Refuge, which Rendel commenced in 1849, and is now in course of construction, will enclose this harbour, as well as a great part of the bay, or about 320 acres, with deep water, not less than 6 fathoms, throughout, and room for 400 sail. The principal breakwater, that to the north, will be 5,000 feet long, 170 broad, and 30 above the bottom of the sea, in the deepest part. A smaller one, or pier, will be 2,100 feet long, and broad. These run out towards the Platter Rocks, having a width of three quarters of a mile, and are built of solid stone, from the Holyhead Hill to the west of the town, which is 710 feet high to the camp at top (Caer Gybi), and from which a tram rail brings down 25,000 tons of that material a week. The rock is schistus quartz, dislodged by galvanic explosions, and about 6,000,000 tons have been already sunk into the sea. The works were visited by the Queen and Prince Albert in 1853.

All this coast is worth visiting; excursions may be made to the following: On the west side of Holyhead Hill are the North and South Stack Rocks, hollowed into caves and swarming with wild birds. The Parliament Cave in the north stack is 70 feet high. On the south stack is a lighthouse 200 feet high, built in 1809, joined to the mainland by a small suspension bridge 110 feet long, towards which you descend the face of the cliff by the Stairs, 380 steps, altogether. The rock is frequently variegated, or greasy to the touch, like soapstone. The rail, on its way to Bangor, passes near the south coast of Anglesey, where you may inspect the curious little churches of Llangwffen and Llanddwyn, each on an island; also Aberffraw the decayed capital of the early North Wales princes, and Bodorgan, a seat of the Meyricks. From Holyhead, along the north coast, you pass Skerries Light, on a dreary rock: till 1835 it belonged to a private person, who sold it to the Trinity Board for £445,000! Such was the enormous revenue derived from passing ships. Then the three Mouse Rocks, off Cemmaes Bay, where the *Olinda* steamer was wrecked in 1854, in her passage outward from Liverpool. The rocks are high here. Next comes Amlwch, which has a harbour cut out of the slaty cliffs, for exporting copper from the famous Pary's Mine, first worked in March, 1768, and worth at one time £300,000 a year. It is in the side of a hill, 2 miles south of the town. Lead and silver are also found; and there are factories for alum and vitriol, from the sulphate of copper.

Holyhead Harbour or Refuge. As the shortest and most direct route from London to Dublin, the passage via Holyhead has always engaged the attention of Government;

so that before the introduction of railways, they had caused to be formed one of the finest mail-coach roads in the kingdom: this great work, executed by Telford, the renowned engineer, in the beginning of the present century, was considered his chef d'oeuvre, with the graceful suspension bridge spanning the Menai Straits, and the road terminating in Holyhead, at what is now called the Old Harbour, from whence sailing packets, carrying the mails, took their departure direct for Kingstown (Dublin). The next road brought to bear upon this port, with the same object (that of shortening the distance as much as possible between the two capitals), was an iron one; and the Chester and Holyhead Railway Company, with a spirit and energy commensurate with the object to be obtained; overcame all difficulties; and, with Mr Peto (now Sir S. M. Peto, Bart.) as their indefatigable chairman, and Mr Stephenson as their engineer, they constructed the now world-known Britannia Tubular Bridge, through which the mails and passengers from London rapidly pass, at a level of 100 feet above the tide, then across the island of Anglesey to Holyhead Harbour, where the Company's and Mail Steam Packets are waiting to receive them, and a sea passage of four hours and a half (the 64 miles intervening) lands them in safety in Ireland.

The increasing importance of this station, together with its applicability, induced the Board of Admiralty to select this spot for the formation of one of the national Harbours of Refuge, and that work is now being carried out. The harbour is formed by a breakwater to the northward, about 5,000 feet in length, leaving the shore in the form of a bent arm extending outwards from Soldier's Point and the Platter's Buoy; and another pier running out from the opposite shore, or Salt Island, eastward, a distance of 2,000 feet: these two arms enclosing an area 316 acres, three quarters of a mile long, and with a depth of 6 or 7 fathoms, at low water, will when completed, make one of the finest artificial refuge barbours and packet stations in the world.

The once small town of Holyhead, situated in a remote corner of Anglesey, will speedily become an important place. Already we have shown the continual attention given to it, as lying in the direct route from London to Dublin (which traffic and communication the London and North Western Company is year by year increasing and developing); and, when the new harbour is completed the town will still rise more into importance from having been selected as the point for carrying out a work of which England may well be proud – a harbour achieved on a most dangerous and unprotected coast, offering a free shelter to vessels of every nation, and a haven of refuge to the mariner of every flag.

Holyhead to Dublin

The passage across from Holyhead to Kingstown, a distance of 64 miles, is now generally performed in 4 to 6 hours, and the traveller has scarcely lost sight of the mountains of Carnarvon before those of Dublin and Wicklow become visible.